AVOIDING TRIVIA

AVOIDING TRIVIA

The Role of Strategic Planning in American Foreign Policy

DANIEL W. DREZNER

editor

BROOKINGS INSTITUTION PRESS
Washington, D.C.

Copyright © 2009
THE BROOKINGS INSTITUTION
1775 Massachusetts Avenue, N.W., Washington, D.C. 20036
www.brookings.edu

Library of Congress Cataloging-in-Publication data

Avoiding trivia : the role of strategic planning in American foreign policy / Daniel W. Drezner, editor.
    p. cm.
  Includes bibliographical references and index.
  Summary: "Critically assesses the past, future, and potential future role and impact of long-term strategic planning in foreign policy. Key figures from past decades of foreign policy and planning provide authoritative insight on the difficulties and importance of thinking and acting in a coherent way for the long term"—Provided by publisher.
  ISBN 978-0-8157-0306-8 (pbk. : alk. paper)
  1. United States—Foreign relations—Planning. 2. Strategic planning—United States. I. Drezner, Daniel W. II. Title.
  JZ1480.A987 2009
  327.73—dc22   2009012069

9 8 7 6 5 4 3 2 1

The paper used in this publication meets minimum requirements of the American National Standard for Information Sciences—Permanence of Paper for Printed Library Materials: ANSI Z39.48-1992.

Typeset in Minion

Composition by Cynthia Stock
Silver Spring, Maryland

Printed by R. R. Donnelley
Harrisonburg, Virginia

Contents

Acknowledgments

The year 2007 marked the sixtieth anniversary of the creation of the State Department's policy planning staff, and the seventy-fifth anniversary of the founding of the Fletcher School of Law and Diplomacy at Tufts University. To commemorate both events, I organized a conference in April 2008 entitled "The Past, Present, and Future of Policy Planning." More than twenty scholars and policymakers participated in the two-day conference, including five former heads of the State Department's policy planning staff. The roundtables and discussions proved to be so stimulating that a consensus quickly emerged to produce this edited volume.

Getting from a conference idea to a finished book requires a great deal of assistance. I am grateful to all of the participants in the conference at Fletcher. In addition to the contributors to this volume, Stephen Bosworth, James Lindsay, P. J. Crowley, Tom Malinowski, Meghan O'Sullivan, Peter Rodman, Gideon Rose, Mary Sarotte, Robert Schulzinger, James Steinberg, and Jeffrey Taliaferro provided valuable insight and feedback. The Carnegie Foundation and Cabot Family Charitable Trust provided the necessary funding for the conference to take place, and I am therefore most grateful to Carnegie's Steven Del Rosso and Cabot's John Cabot for making this possible. Karen Mollung organized all of the conference logistics, and thanks to her, everything ran on time. Katherine Pattillo, Jennifer Buntman, Zack Gold, Joe Gagliano, James Palmer, and MacKinnon Webster provided invaluable support as well. The administration at Fletcher—in particular Stephen Bosworth, Gerald Sheehan, Roger Milici, and George Kosar—left me with only the smallest of managerial details.

I thank Jen Weedon, Dahlia Shaham, and Margaret Riden for their indispensable research assistance and value added during the final stages of putting this volume together. Any value subtracted from this volume because of errors and omissions rests firmly on my shoulders. At the Brookings Institution Press, Chris Kelaher handled the review process, and Janet Walker oversaw the copyediting with efficiency and dispatch. All of the contributors appreciate the constructive remarks made by the two anonymous referees.

Aaron Friedberg's chapter originally appeared in the Winter 2007/08 issue of the *Washington Quarterly*. I am grateful to the Center for Strategic and International Studies and MIT Press for allowing its publication in this volume. A shortened version of my introductory chapter appeared in the Winter 2009 issue of the *Fletcher Forum on World Affairs*.

Introduction

PART

I

DANIEL W. DREZNER

1

The Challenging Future of Strategic Planning in Foreign Policy

"Avoid trivia."

—Secretary of State George Marshall's advice to
George Kennan, the first director of policy planning

Strategic planning for American foreign policy is dead, dying, or moribund. This, at least, has been the assessment of several commentators and policy-makers in recent years.[1] Michèle Flournoy and Shawn Brimley observed in 2006, "For a country that continues to enjoy an unrivaled global position, it is both remarkable and disturbing that the United States has no truly effective strategic planning process for national security."[2] At an academic conference in 2007, a former director of the State Department's policy planning staff complained that, "six years after 9/11, we still don't have a grand strategy." Aaron Friedberg, who was director of policy planning for Vice President Richard Cheney, writes in this volume, "The U.S. government has lost the capacity to conduct serious, sustained national strategic planning." Admiral William Fallon, the CENTCOM commander until the spring of 2008, told the *New York Times* that the United States would need to focus more on policy planning: "We need to have a well-thought-out game plan for engagement in the world that we adjust regularly and that has some system of checks and balances built into it."[3] In this volume, Council on Foreign Relations president Richard Haass argues that the United States has "squandered" its post–cold war opportunity, concluding, "Historians will not judge the United States well for how it has used these twenty years."

These sorts of laments have become common in the past decade, in no small part because of the foreign policy planning of the administrations of Bill

Clinton and George W. Bush. Members of the Clinton administration's foreign policy team prided themselves on their ad hoc approach to foreign policy problems.[4] The Bush administration had ambitious policy goals, but failed to develop the plans and policies necessary to achieve them.[5] The challenges facing President Barack Obama in 2009 are stark: a malaise in strategic planning has fed a nostalgia for the days of George Kennan and his founding of the State Department's policy planning staff.[6]

What, exactly, is strategic planning? In his memoirs, Secretary of State Dean Acheson provided one useful definition: "to look ahead, not into the distant future, but beyond the vision of the operating officers caught in the smoke and crises of current battle; far enough ahead to see the emerging form of things to come and outline what should be done to meet or anticipate them." Acheson thought that policy planners should also "constantly reappraise" existing policies.[7] That view matches how the contributors to this volume use the term. Strategic planning is not limited to grand strategy; it can apply to regional and crisis situations as well. It should also be noted that strategic or policy planning is not just about top-down implementation.[8] It can also be about reinterpreting past and current actions through a new analytic lens, one that carries "heuristic punch," as Stephen Krasner phrases it in his chapter.

As the contributors to this volume suggest, there are three ways in which strategic planning affects foreign policy: through the plans, the planning, and the planners. If the policy plans are actually implemented, their effect on foreign affairs is self-evident. Even if they are not implemented, however, the process matters as well. Planning is not limited to plans; it is also about the patterns of thinking that best match resources and capabilities to achieving the desired policy ends. Similarly, if the planners are thought to be capable and strategically minded, then they will be more likely to influence responses to new and unanticipated events. Even when plans are OBE—overtaken by events—the process and the individuals are still important.

In foreign policy, the concept of strategic planning is synonymous with the State Department's policy planning staff—or "S/P" as it is called within the confines of Foggy Bottom. During its sixty-year history, the actual functions of the staff have varied widely, ranging from speech-writing duties to operational functions to acting as a liaison to the foreign policy community outside of the government. Its mission is highly unusual in twenty-first-century American government. According to its own website, the goal of S/P is "to take a longer term, strategic view of global trends and frame recommendations for the Secretary of State to advance U.S. interests and American values."[9] This goes against the grain of a 24/7, real-time, rapid-reaction era in which policymakers define the long term as anything longer than a week. Part of the challenge of twenty-first-century foreign policy is to think about how this concept should be applied to all foreign policy agencies.

Demand for cogent strategic planning has not been matched by scholarly interest in the subject. In one respect, this is not surprising. The glamour of grand strategy will always trump debates about the processes that enable or retard policy planning. Certainly in the academic study of international relations, grand theory is accorded greater respect than foreign policy analysis. Simply put, everyone likes debating the content of the plans themselves more than the bureaucratic plumbing behind the plans. In another respect, however, previous decades saw at least *some* scholarly interest in this topic.[10] In recent years, however, there has been very little research on this subject.[11] This volume hopes to address this gap.

With a new presidential administration comes a hope that strategic planning—within and outside the State Department—will play an elevated role. At a time when the United States faces a rising number of foreign policy challenges, the need for planning would appear to be greater than ever. Are strategic planners housed in the Pentagon, State Department, Treasury Department, National Security Council, and National Intelligence Council capable of rising to the challenge? Indeed, is strategic planning a viable concept in the twenty-first century?

These are the questions that animate this volume. Future policymakers need to comprehend the utility and the limits of policy planning. This introduction sets the stage by discussing the external, internal, and historical challenges that policy principals face in adapting the strategic planning process to meet the challenges of the here and now. Externally, the United States faces a plethora of complex and overlapping challenges that would seem to require an even greater emphasis on strategic planning. Internally, the wars of this century have contributed to an unbalanced mix of foreign policy resources—a material fact that hampers coordination of the policy planning process. Historically, the imposing—and inflated—legacy of George Kennan has cast a formidable shadow over his successors. This complicates an already challenging task: balancing the inherent tension between strategic planning and operational authority in the crafting of foreign policy.

External Challenges

With the passing of the George W. Bush presidency, there is a demand for new concepts and plans to organize American foreign policy. Containment is dead and gone. The Bush doctrine was unpopular at home and abroad.[12] Isolationism is simply not a viable option. Both policymakers and scholars need a better grasp of how to craft viable, long-term strategies for the twenty-first century.

To describe the current international environment as complex would be an understatement. To appreciate the depth of the external challenges, consider the Princeton Project on National Security, a multiyear, multipronged effort to develop a twenty-first-century doctrine that could achieve what containment accomplished during the cold war. The effort to create a "Kennan by committee" involved hundreds of foreign policy analysts. But after dozens of meetings, the final report concluded, "It became clear that such an organizing principle—such as containment, enlargement, balancing or democracy promotion—would not be forthcoming. Indeed, no overarching concept fit because no one danger facing the United States is the overarching threat."[13] If today's leading foreign policy analysts cannot agree on a single heuristic to anchor U.S. foreign policy, policy planning becomes that much more difficult (though not impossible, as Tom Wright discusses in his chapter).

It is easy to list the external challenges facing the United States. From a conventional, state-centric perspective, the greatest one is coping with the rise of developing country great powers. In 2006 the *National Journal* ran a cover story resuscitating Paul Kennedy's thesis of America's "imperial overstretch," articulated most prominently in *The Rise and Fall of the Great Powers*. Kennedy's assessment of the current situation was stark: "There are now more players on the globe who can screw us rather more effectively than we can screw them."[14] Today the trend lines only reinforce that assessment, even among America's allies. In 2007 the French foreign minister declared that "the magic is over" for America's image, and the German finance minister declared that the United States would soon lose its status as a financial superpower.[15] The global financial crisis has, if anything, brought these subterranean pressures into the foreground.

Power is a relative measure, and the United States is in relative decline because of the astonishing growth rates and capital surpluses of the developing world. Among the rising powers, China and India stand out. China possesses two trillion dollars in hard-currency reserves, and is starting to use its financial muscle to achieve foreign policy objectives.[16] India's high-tech sector is growing by leaps and bounds. Both countries are nuclear powers that aspire to have blue-water navies. To date their ascent has been impressive, but the future is what grabs everyone's attention. By 2020 the National Intelligence Council projects that China and India will have the world's second and fourth largest economies.[17] Simple extrapolations from the recent past can be misleading. Nevertheless, economic and demographic trends suggest that the growth of India and China will push world politics into a new multipolar era.

The growth of these states is a challenge unto itself, but it also highlights a related problem. The tectonic shift in world politics further weakens the international institutions that were previously thought to "matter." The United States helped establish a bevy of global governance structures between 1945 and 1955: the United Nations, International Monetary Fund, World Bank, General Agreement on Tariffs and Trade (GATT), North Atlantic Treaty Organization (NATO), Organization for Economic Cooperation and Development (OECD), and others. As long as the United States and its allies were the most important actors in the world, these institutions served the twin purpose of coordinating and legitimizing the global rules of the game. As the distribution of power in the world shifts, however, the United States needs to think about how to revamp these institutions in order to maintain their relevance. To its credit, the Bush administration recognized this problem, but its efforts at addressing it were fitful.[18] A decade of global governance reform efforts has yielded little in the way of concrete results.[19] Key institutions—like the G-8 and the World Trade Organization (WTO)—are in danger of becoming overwhelmed by a spaghetti bowl of newer arrangements.[20] A 2008 *Foreign Affairs* essay recommended that the United States and its Western allies simply get out of the way and let the developing world have its turn at global governance.[21]

Handling a power transition is tricky, but handling it while simultaneously coping with a rise in systemic threats is even trickier. Concerns about terrorism and weapons of mass destruction will, for obvious reasons, remain near the top of the list. Of related concern is the growth of nonstate actors, like Hamas and Hezbollah, that appear to be more powerful than the territorial governments in which they are based. Just as the balance of power is shifting away from the United States, power is also shifting from states to nonstate actors. Richard Haass warns about the rise in "nonpolarity"—the ebbing of power from governments to more amorphous, networked actors; Niall Ferguson makes a similar claim when he talks about "apolarity."[22] Others have observed the rise of superempowered individuals who have amassed influence in world politics.[23] The U.S. government will need to figure out how best to interface with these new kinds of foreign policy actors.

The most novel threats, however, are even more nontraditional in nature. In the 2008 calendar year, global markets in financial assets, food, and energy were buffeted by a series of shocks, and none of them functioned terribly well in response. In all three sectors, national governments responded with greater intervention. It is far from clear, however, whether these interventions will be welfare-enhancing on any level. Beyond the failures of global markets, there are additional concerns. Global warming will increasingly insert itself into the international policy agenda. The specter of a global disease pandemic remains ever-present.

It would be dangerous to exaggerate the challenges posed to the United States. As David Gordon and Daniel Twining observe in their contribution to this volume, American primacy has yet to disappear. By many metrics, American power remains unparalleled.[24] Despite claims of global anti-Americanism, surveys demonstrate that the United States possesses large reservoirs of soft power in the Pacific Rim.[25] The relative decline of the United States is not likely to be as dramatic as, say, the decline and fall of the British empire.[26]

America's external adversaries have their own problems and policy reversals. As of this writing, it is abundantly clear that Al Qaeda is facing even greater challenges. It is suffering from strong ideological rejection and push-back in the Middle East—even among those sympathetic to the idea of jihad.[27] Intelligence analysis reveals that the terrorist group, like the sovereign governments it battles, suffers from bureaucratic sclerosis and petty infighting.[28] Following a raft of books hailing China as *the* challenger to American hegemony, Beijing in 2008 suffered an *annus horribilis* of health and safety scares, foreign policy blowback in Africa, erratic and unstable allies on its border, ecological catastrophe, natural disasters, and a dramatic economic downturn.

Despite these caveats, the trend line is disturbing. The distribution of power is shifting away from the United States, as is the distribution of preferences. The Washington Consensus is now a dead letter, and American values seem less enticing than they did a decade ago. Simply put, at the end of 2008 the United States generated less respect, less influence, less goodwill, less standing, and less relative power in world politics than it did at any time during the post–cold war era.[29]

Internal Challenges

Dissatisfaction with the status quo does not guarantee that there will be a change of tack. There are several internal constraints that make it difficult to improve strategic planning. Part of the problem rests with the incomplete search for new strategic ideas. As Jeffrey Legro points out in his chapter, a lot is required to revamp American foreign policy.[30] There needs to be a viable alternative around which others can rally—one that can generate immediately attractive solutions to current problems. During George W. Bush's second term, a number of scholars and ex-policymakers tried to devise new and attractive grand strategies.[31] The result was a pulling and hauling in different directions. These ideas have different labels—progressive realism, realistic Wilsonianism, ethical realism, liberal realism—and their creators hoped to earn fame, fortune, or perhaps a spot on the Obama administration's foreign policy team. Until the foreign policy machinery of an administration develops a consensus choice for a new alternative, existing policy will remain in effect.

There are other internal reasons for the malaise in policy planning, however. Persistent pathologies in American foreign policy make strategic planning difficult. As Richard Haass recounts in his chapter, bureaucratic politics can make rational planning a difficult process. Haass's policy planning staff developed the original draft of the 2002 National Security Strategy, but then lost control over the drafting process to the National Security Council (NSC). In their chapter, Peter Feaver and William Inboden hint that rising levels of partisan rancor have made it more difficult to engage in dispassionate strategic planning.

A significant factor is the growing imbalance of foreign policy resources among the relevant bureaucracies. Consider the previous two administrations. During the Clinton years, both the State and Defense Department budgets were cut significantly in real dollar terms, as was foreign aid. By the end of the Clinton years, the Treasury Department was widely viewed as the most important agency in American foreign policy.[32] There were myriad reasons for this. Foreign economic policy became increasingly important as barriers to goods and capital fell and global economic interdependence increased. Treasury's access to resources, however, played a significant part as well.

This lopsidedness increased in the Bush years, although in a radically different direction. The global war on terror and the war in Iraq led to vast increases in the Defense Department budget.[33] To comprehend the extent of this mismatch, consider that the musicians in U.S. military marching bands outnumber the entire Foreign Service.[34] Indeed, the mismatch got so bad that in 2007, Defense Secretary Robert Gates publicly pleaded for more resources—for the civilian foreign policy agencies: "There is a need for a dramatic increase in spending on the civilian instruments of national security—diplomacy, strategic communications, foreign assistance, civic action, and economic reconstruction and development. . . . We must focus our energies beyond the guns and steel of the military, beyond just our brave soldiers, sailors, Marines, and airmen. We must also focus our energies on the other elements of national power that will be so crucial in the coming years."[35] When one agency head lobbies hard for another agency's budget, it signals that resource allocation in foreign policy is seriously askew.

How do operational budgets affect policy planning? In theory, operational control over resources should not matter. In practice, a cardinal rule of bureaucratic politics is that organizations that command greater staff and resources are more likely to get their way in policy implementation. As Stephen Krasner, Andrew Erdmann, and Amy Zegart observe in their chapters, emergent strategies and plans emanate from actions already taken. The agencies that have the greatest resources will be able to act first, creating path dependencies and lock-ins from which planning units might never escape. No wonder Gates warned in 2008 about the "creeping militarization" of American foreign policy.[36]

The agencies that command significant resources will inevitably dictate the policy planning process. During the Asian financial crisis, Treasury had the lead in formulating a policy response, despite the obvious security externalities of the meltdown.[37] This was due in part to Treasury's growing expertise, while State faced increasing difficulty holding on to its top personnel.[38]

Similarly, during the last years of the Bush administration, the military began flexing more muscle in the allocation of foreign aid and the coordination of regional policies. The U.S. Southern Command, for example, issued a "Command Strategy 2016" document, in which it conceived itself as the lead agency coordinating civilian and military resources in the region—despite the fact that the Command did not envision any armed combat scenarios in the region.[39] As one assessment of this report concluded, "The sheer number of U.S. military personnel engaged in Latin America, and the resources that the Southern Command has available, makes them the elephant in the room. *They dominate what they coordinate*" (emphasis added).[40] A former Bush administration official acknowledged that, "while serving the State Department . . . over the past four years, I witnessed firsthand the quiet, de facto military takeover of much of the U.S. government."[41]

The challenge for policy planning is the ability of these units to balance planning and operational roles. Kennan himself concluded that the fundamental constraint on policy planning was "the impossibility of having the planning function performed outside of the line of command. . . . The operating units—the geographical and functional units—will not take interference from any unit outside the line of command."[42] Policy planning directors have handled this challenge in different ways. Some have insisted on maximizing "face time" with policy principals to ensure continued access—traveling with the secretary of state on overseas trips, for example. Others have acquired operational as well as planning functions. Richard Haass, for example, was given ambassadorial rank and put in charge of the Northern Ireland peace process. It remains unclear, however, whether these tactics have an appreciable effect on policy.

The resource asymmetry, and the persistent tension between planning and operations, suggests a disturbing paradox about the future of policy planning. Ideally, the policy planning process should be able to determine the proper sequencing and allocation of foreign policy resources. The imbalance in existing resources, however, empowers some agencies at the expense of others. This imbalance threatens to warp the existing process in a way that guarantees a suboptimal outcome.

One possible way to correct this problem is to create a smooth interagency process that handles policy planning. In its waning months, the Bush administration issued a National Security Presidential Directive to formalize the interagency strategic planning process into a National Security Policy Planning Committee. This committee includes the policy planning heads of the National Security Council, National Intelligence Council, Joint Chiefs of Staff, and the Departments of State, Defense, Treasury, Justice, and Homeland Security.

The problem is that the planning units outside the State Department have had a more precarious existence. Offices of strategic planning have a more intermittent history in the Pentagon, the National Security Council, and the Treasury Department.[43] Without greater stability of the planning bureaucracy, better interagency coordination will be difficult, at best, to achieve. Bruce Jentleson suggests, in his chapter, a more integrated executive branch–wide effort to engage in better strategic planning.

A related question is which planning agency should have the "lead" in such a coordination process. Historically, S/P has the greatest institutional memory and legacy in these matters. However, Aaron Friedberg, Bruce Jentleson, and Peter Feaver and William Inboden argue that the center of gravity in foreign policymaking has shifted over the past sixty years. Over the decades the president has supplanted the secretary of state as the principal foreign policy official. By that logic, Friedberg posits that the central organizer for strategic planning should be housed within the White House. Feaver and Inboden make the case for embedding a strategic planning unit within the National Security Council. Jentleson argues in favor of a Strategic Planning Inter-Agency Group, coordinated by the NSC. As Amy Zegart observes, however, the iron laws of bureaucratic politics suggest that such reform efforts will come to naught.

One timeless suggestion is to reform government institutions to make them more like the private sector. Some reformers suggest that if government policy planning copied techniques from private firms, the U.S. government would improve its grand strategy. Andrew Erdmann, however, dissents from this view. Having worked at both S/P and the private sector, he points out that corporations can neglect their strategic planning units just as much as the federal government.

Historical Challenges

James Steinberg was the director of policy planning from March 1994 to December 1996. He tells the following story about his first day as the policy planning director. He went to his new office and found the portraits of all the former directors hanging on the walls. As Steinberg looked at them, he came to a stunning realization. Even though the office had been in existence for close to half a century, every single former director was still alive. For a moment, Steinberg was convinced that he had discovered the secret to immortality!

Steinberg's anecdote is amusing but also revealing. The mythology that surrounds strategic planning stretches back to Kennan and his formidable intellectual shadow. Under the first heads of S/P—Kennan, Paul Nitze, and Robert Bowie—the policy planning staff played a pivotal role in developing the Marshall Plan, NATO, the Korean War strategy, nuclear policy, the response to the Suez crisis, and plans for the European economic recovery.[44] The success of these policies has encouraged Kennan's successors to aim just as high.

The problem is that it is far from clear whether policy planners can still possess Kennan's influence. Many contributors to this volume observe that the first few directors had the greatest influence over American foreign policy. This view matches the historical consensus. Twenty years ago, Lucian Pugliaresi and Diane Berliner noted, "S/P no longer commands a dominant position in the development of U.S. foreign policy."[45] Recent initiatives have yielded mixed results. Morton Halperin, for example, used the office to initiate efforts at democracy promotion. Halperin's Community of Democracies project is essentially moribund. Time will tell whether Stephen Krasner's Partnership for Democratic Governance faces a similar fate.

Does this mean that current staffers at policy planning agencies cannot match the accomplishments of their predecessors? Hardly. The conditions for policy planning to play a significant role go far beyond individual ability. The success of policy planning units depends crucially on the interpersonal relationships of policy principals. The historical consensus is that George Kennan, Paul Nitze, Robert Bowie, Winston Lord, and Dennis Ross stand out as "making a difference" at S/P. While these individuals were and are able statesmen, it is far from clear that their talents outshine those of other former directors, such as W. W. Rostow, Anthony Lake, Paul Wolfowitz, Morton Halperin, or Richard Haass.

A key difference between these two groups was in the relationship between themselves and the secretary of state, and the relationship between the secretary and the president. The first four directors had the confidence of their bosses (George Marshall, Dean Acheson, John Foster Dulles, Henry Kissinger, James Baker). Kennan, for example, was the only State Department official to have unfettered access to George Marshall's office. These secretaries of state, in turn, earned the trust of presidents that were engaged in foreign policy (Truman, Eisenhower, Nixon, and George H. W. Bush). The same cannot be said of the latter group of policy planning directors, who had to negotiate more troublesome relationships between their policy principals (Rusk/Kennedy, Vance/Carter, Haig/Reagan, Albright/Clinton, and Powell/Bush). The best policy planning staff in the world will have little influence unless it lucks its way into a favorable bureaucratic and political environment.[46]

It is worth remembering that although current analysts look back on the late 1940s as the halcyon era of policy planning, Kennan himself took a much dimmer view. When he decided to resign in November 1949, he wrote in his diary, "It is time I recognized that my Policy Planning Staff, started nearly three years ago, has simply been a failure, like all previous attempts to bring order and foresight into the designing of foreign policy by special institutional arrangements."[47] Indeed, as several of the contributors to this volume observe, the doctrine of containment as implemented by Nitze and his successors looked very different from Kennan's original conception. Thomas Wright points out that Kennan opposed the creation of NATO, the most successful alliance in world history. Indeed, for all of his analytical brilliance, Kennan erred in many of his predictions and evinced little understanding of the country he served. It would serve those involved in policy planning to respect Kennan's intellect, without lapsing into hagiography.

Even when the institutional and interpersonal conditions do not exist for policy planning to excel, they can exist in the future. As Stephen Krasner observes, crisis, change, and uncertainty can provide an agenda-setting moment when none previously existed.[48] Consider, for example, the "responsible stakeholder" language currently used toward China. According to Krasner, an S/P staff member originally conceived this idea and put it into a policy planning paper in early 2003. It was submitted and subsequently ignored by higher-ups. With a change in personnel after January 2005, the same staff member resubmitted the same paper. The second time around,

Deputy Secretary of State Robert Zoellick embraced the concept and adopted it as his own.

If luck is the residue of design, then perhaps the best advice for policy planners is to be fully prepared for the moment when the right policy principles and the right circumstances fuse individual thought with American action. This goes back to the distinction between plans and planning. While the plans themselves might not always matter, the planning process is indispensable.

The Rest of This Volume

The contributors to this volume represent the proud tradition of scholar-practitioners who have animated American foreign policy since the end of the Second World War. They do not agree on everything, however. Richard Haass argues that the focus should be on policy design rather than divining the future. Others devote considerable space to anticipating the future. Expectations about the possibility of reform also vary. Bruce Jentleson and Aaron Friedberg advocate reforms that they believe are feasible. Amy Zegart and Stephen Krasner are more skeptical about the prospects for changing the current system. Rather than trying to reconcile these contrasting views, readers are invited to reach their own conclusions.

Strategic planning requires a familiarity with the environment in which one is planning. The first group of chapters peers into the strategic and political environment for the United States in order to characterize the challenges for policy planners. Richard Haass, director of the State Department Policy Planning Staff from 2001 to 2003 and now president of the Council on Foreign Relations, considers whether policy planning is possible in today's strategic environment. He discusses both bureaucratic and organizational challenges as well as conditions peculiar to the international environment. He argues that a number of policy areas are ripe for attention and offers both substantive and operational guidance to the next administration's policy planners. Noting strains on U.S. military and financial resources, he argues that the tools most readily available to the next administration will be diplomatic. Haass concludes that today's domestic and international conditions make policy planning not only possible, but necessary.

David Gordon and Daniel Twining (Bush's last director of policy planning and an S/P staff member, respectively) examine the key long-term threats to American power and presence in the international system. They argue that the challenges facing the United States today are more diffuse and, in a very real sense, will require the effective use of all elements of national power, including skillful diplomacy. Nevertheless, they argue that the United States is well placed to meet these challenges and to thrive in the twenty-first-century international system. Over the next few decades, they say, "American power and influence will be buffeted by three key long-term challenges: violent extremism, the rise of Asia, and the economic and information revolutions of globalization." However, they maintain that "the United States will remain indispensable to the world economy, international security, and the management of relations among the great powers. There will be challengers. But there is no peer competitor that can replicate this nation's global position, its strengths as a society, or its leadership. The greatest risks arise not from the emergence of new powers but from their propensity to free-ride: their inability or unwillingness to carry their weight in global governance and the provision of international public goods, on which the international system remains disproportionately dependent on the United States."

Jeffrey Legro considers whether there will be major change in U.S. foreign policy once the campaign rhetoric has died down. He believes it to be unlikely. The United States, after the brief experimentation with the Bush doctrine, has returned to the basic "American Internationalism" foreign policy agenda that guided the United States between 1946 and 2001. There remains widespread support for continuing that agenda, featuring U.S. international leadership, military superiority, support for democracies abroad, free trade, and multilateralism. To be sure, Legro argues, there will ABB (anything but Bush) adaptations in policy, especially in the Middle East, but even the Bush administration itself had already returned to the U.S. postwar tradition by about 2005. Legro identifies a deeper problem: the growing friction between the American Supremacy view and emerging international conditions. This friction will lead to mounting pressure for change. Yet what is still absent in the United States is a worldview that has enough social support to replace the current one. Policy planning in the years ahead therefore will involve (1) implementing the neo-American Internationalism, (2) attending to failed expectations, and (3) planning for an alternative set of strategic principles.

The next group of chapters addresses how strategic planning can best be implemented and reformed within the executive branch. Bruce Jentleson argues for a better executive branch–wide process, systematically integrating policy planning across State, Defense, the intelligence community, Treasury, and other key departments and agencies and structurally linking them to the National Security Council. The challenges—analytic, organizational, political—of designing such an integrative executive branch strategy are not to be underestimated. Nor, though, is the need. Jentleson makes the substantive policy case, given the complexity of the foreign policy agenda and the corresponding need to integrate the perspectives and capacities of the full range of key executive branch entities. He then proposes a strategy for a new administration, both structurally and substantively.

Aaron Friedberg argues that the absence of a coherent policy planning process within the executive branch raises the risk of "catastrophic failure." Although the problem is structural, and no perfect solution exists, he believes that significant improvements are possible. He proposes three possible reforms: reviving the Eisenhower-era Planning Board, creating a National Security Council strategic planning directorate, or inserting a permanent strategic planning cell within the NSC.

In President Bush's second term, National Security Adviser Stephen Hadley implemented aspects of Friedberg's latter two options. He increased the capacity for strategic planning at the NSC with a new office: the office of the Special Adviser for Strategic Planning and Institutional Reform (SPIR). Peter Feaver and William Inboden were the first SPIR staffers. Feaver and Inboden observe that while the White House is a focal point for strategic planning in national security, it is also a very difficult environment in which to do the kind of step-back analysis required. They argue that SPIR was able to increase substantially the attention the NSC and the White House paid to strategic planning, along the way confirming much of the conventional wisdom about the challenges and opportunities for this function at the top-most level of government. They argue that the record of that office is a useful point of departure for the next administration.

The final group of chapters explores the limitations and opportunities for strategic planning. Amy Zegart casts a skeptical eye on institutional efforts to improve the strategic planning process. She says that all strategic planners face four types of constraints: time pressures to address current issues at the expense of longer-term planning; bureaucratic competition for influence; cognitive barriers to anticipating the future; and cultural tensions between policy planning "thinkers" and policymaking "doers" within the U.S. government. As these constraints continue to grow, she believes that policy planning will be more difficult in this century than in the last one.

Thomas Wright discusses how the United States should draw on the lessons of the past to think about strategic planning for the future. He observes that much of what we think we know about U.S. grand strategy in the 1940s is mistaken. Initially, there was no viable blueprint for postwar order, and what plans there were collapsed in failure. The order that subsequently emerged was ad hoc, and many of the attributes that we value today (such as strategic restraint and self-constraint) were unintended by the founders. Drawing from both early and recent history, Wright outlines key principles for institutional reform as a guide for current strategic planners.

Andrew Erdmann looks at the lessons that can be drawn from private sector examples of strategic planning. The private sector experience with strategic planning is mixed, and there is dissatisfaction with "traditional" models that envision a group of specialized planners devising a strategy that is then implemented. Strategy instead is both deliberate and emergent; it manifests itself in decisions made and actions taken. Erdmann argues that the process should aim to create "prepared minds," not stale prepared plans. Companies have experimented with different approaches to strategy development to inject greater creativity and relevance into the process. Success also requires integration with execution. Thus, Erdmann argues, successful planning is one part of the broader challenge of "strategic management." Private sector experience underscores that the CEO must own and drive strategy, line executives need to be involved in the strategy's development, and last, that strategy staffs should focus on helping others make the strategy, not on devising the strategy themselves. While process matters, business history also reminds us that there is only so much that process can accomplish over the long haul: developing, implementing, and then reinventing successful strategies is a task that few ever achieve.

Finally, Stephen Krasner uses the "garbage can" model of organizational behavior to explain both the limitations and opportunities for policy planners. The best strategies in the world are unimportant if there is no interest among policy principals, or if politics prevents the plan from ever being implemented. Discussing his own experiences as director of policy planning from 2005 to 2007, Krasner recounts the role that opportunity and luck play in implementing policy initiatives. There are moments when policy planning staffs can make critical contributions. The mixture of skills possessed by staff members endows them with a privileged role within the policy alternatives stream. When policy windows do open up, planning staffs are at least one promising source from which new solutions might flow.

Notes

1. In addition to the people quoted below, see Dennis Ross, *Statecraft* (New York: Farrar, Straus & Giroux, 2007); CSIS Commission on Smart Power, *A Smarter, More Secure America* (Washington: Center for Strategic and International Studies, 2007).

2. Michèle Flournoy and Shawn Brimley, "Strategic Planning for National Security," *Joint Force Quarterly* 41 (2nd quarter 2006): 80.

3. Quoted in Elaine Sciolino, "Push for New Direction Leads to Sudden End for a 40-Year Naval Career," *New York Times,* May 31, 2008.

4. David Halberstam, *War in a Time of Peace* (New York: Scribner's, 2001), p. 409; see also Derek Chollet and James Goldgeier, *America between the Wars* (New York: Public Affairs, 2008).

5. See, for example, Nora Bensahel, "Mission Not Accomplished: What Went Wrong with Iraqi Reconstruction," *Journal of Strategic Studies* 29 (June 2006): 453–73.

6. See, for example, Ian Bremmer, "George Kennan's Lessons for the War on Terror," *International Herald Tribune,* March 24, 2005; Ian Lustick, *Trapped in the War on Terror* (University of Pennsylvania Press, 2006); James Goldgeier and Derek Chollet, "The Truman Standard," *American Interest* 1 (Summer 2006): 107–11; Ian Shapiro, *Containment: Rebuilding a Strategy against Global Terror* (Princeton University Press, 2007); Aziz Huq, "The Ghost of George Kennan," *American Prospect,* May 15, 2007; James Goldgeier and Derek Chollet, "Good Riddance to the Bush Doctrine," *Washington Post,* July 13, 2008.

7. Dean Acheson, *Present at the Creation* (New York: W. W. Norton, 1969), p. 214.

8. See the chapters by Wright, Erdmann, and Krasner in this volume, as well as Philip Zelikow, "Foreign Policy Engineering: From Theory to Practice and Back Again," *International Security* 18 (Spring 1994): 143–71.

9. See www.state.gov/s/p/ (June 2008).

10. There was a small boomlet of research during the 1970s, for example. See Robert Rothstein, *Planning, Prediction, and Policy-Making in Foreign Affairs* (Boston: Little, Brown, 1972); Lincoln Bloomfield, "Policy Planning Redefined: What the Planners Really Think," *International Journal* 32 (Autumn/1977): 813–28; Jan Kalicki, "The State Department Policy Planning Process," *International Journal* 32 (Autumn 1977): 850–58; Linda Brady, "Planning for Foreign Policy: A Framework for Analysis," *International Journal* 32 (Autumn 1977): 829–48; Lincoln Bloomfield, "Planning Foreign Policy: Can It Be Done?" *Political Science Quarterly* 93 (Autumn 1978): 369–91.

11. For an exception, see *Comprehensive Strategic Reform* (Washington: Center for the Study of the Presidency, 2001).

12. On home attitudes, see Benjamin I. Page and Marshall Bouton, *The Foreign Policy Disconnect: What Americans Want from Our Leaders but Don't Get* (University of Chicago Press, 2006); and Daniel W. Drezner, "The Realist Tradition in American Public Opinion," *Perspectives on Politics* 6 (March 2008): 51–70. On foreign attitudes, see Andrew Kohut and Bruce Stokes, *America against the World: How We Are Different and Why We Are Disliked* (New York: Times Books, 2006).

13. G. John Ikenberry and Anne-Marie Slaughter, *Forging a World of Liberty under Law: U.S. National Security in the 21st Century* (Princeton, N.J.: Princeton Project for National Security, 2006), p. 58.

14. Quoted in Paul Starobin, "Beyond Hegemony," *National Journal,* December 1, 2006.

15. Alison Smale, "'Magic Is Over' for U.S., Says French Foreign Minister," *International Herald Tribune,* March 12, 2008; Bertrand Benoit, "U.S. 'Will Lose Financial Superpower Status.'" *Financial Times,* September 25, 2008.

16. Jamil Anderlini, "Beijing Uses Forex Reserves to Target Taiwan," *Financial Times,* September 11, 2008. See more generally Brad Setser, *Sovereign Wealth and Sovereign Power* (Washington: Council on Foreign Relations Special Report no. 37, September 2008).

17. National Intelligence Council, *Mapping the Global Future* (Washington: Government Printing Office, 2004).

18. Daniel W. Drezner, "The New New World Order," *Foreign Affairs* 86 (March/April 2007): 34–46.

19. Colin Bradford and Johannes Linn, eds., *Global Governance Reform: Breaking the Stalemate* (Washington: Brookings, 2007).

20. Jagdish Bhagwati, *Termites in the Trading System* (Oxford University Press, 2008).

21. Kishore Mahbubani, "The Case against the West," *Foreign Affairs* 87 (May/June 2008): 111–25. .

22. Richard Haass, "The Age of Nonpolarity," *Foreign Affairs* 87 (May/June 2008): 44–56; Niall Ferguson, "A World without Power," *Foreign Policy* (July/August 2004): 32–39.

23. David Rothkopf, *Superclass* (New York: Farrar, Straus & Giroux, 2008); Daniel W. Drezner, "Foreign Policy Goes Glam," *National Interest* 92 (November/December 2007): 22–29.

24. Robert Lieber, "Falling Upwards: Declinism, the Box Set," *World Affairs* 1 (Summer 2008): 48–56.

25. Christopher Whitney and David Shambaugh, *Soft Power in Asia: Results of a Multinational Survey of Public Opinion* (Chicago: Chicago Council on Global Affairs, 2008).

26. Fareed Zakaria, "The Future of American Power," *Foreign Affairs* 87 (May/June 2008): 18–43.

27. For quantitative evidence, see Human Security Brief 2007, May 21, 2008 (www.humansecuritybrief.info/ [December 7, 2008]). For qualitative evidence, see Peter Bergen and Paul Cruickshank, "The Unraveling," *New Republic,* June 11, 2008; Lawrence Wright, "The Rebellion Within," *New Yorker,* June 2, 2008; George Friedman, *Oil and the Saudi Peace Offensive* (Austin, Tex.: Stratfor, June 2, 2008).

28. Joseph Feltzer and Brian Fishman, *Al Qai'da's Foreign Fighters in Iraq: A First Look at the Sinjar Records* (West Point: Combating Terrorism Center, 2008) (www.ctc.usma.edu/harmony/pdf/CTCForeignFighter.19.Dec07.pdf [May 2008]); Sebastian Rotella, "Penalty for Crossing Al Qaeda? A Nasty Memo," *Los Angeles Times,* April 16, 2008.

29. David E. Sanger, *The Inheritance: The World Obama Confronts and the Challenges to American Power* (New York: Harmony Books, 2009).

30. See also Jeffrey Legro, *Rethinking the World: Great Power Strategies and International Order* (Princeton University Press, 2005).

31. For a cursory review, see Daniel W. Drezner, "The Grandest Strategy of Them All," *Washington Post,* December 17, 2006.

32. See David E. Sanger, "Economic Engine for Foreign Policy," *New York Times,* December 28, 2000, p. A1.

33. While the State Department budget also increased during the Bush years, a significant fraction of this increase was dedicated to diplomatic security. See CSIS Commission on Smart Power, *A Smarter, More Secure America,* pp. 63–64.

34. David J. Kilcullen, "New Paradigms for 21st Century Conflict," May 2007 (http://usinfo.state.gov/journals/0507/ijpe/kilcullen.htm [December 8, 2008]).

35. Robert Gates, "Landon Lecture," November 26, 2007 (www.defenselink.mil/speeches/speech.aspx?speechid=1199 [June 2008]).

36. Robert Gates, remarks to the U.S. Global Leadership Campaign, July 15, 2008 (www.defenselink.mil/speeches/speech.aspx?speechid=1262 [July 2008]).

37. See Paul Blustein, *The Chastening* (Washington: Public Affairs, 2001); Robert Rubin and Jacob Weisberg, *In an Uncertain World* (New York: Random House, 2003); Benn Steil and Robert Litan, *Financial Statecraft* (Yale University Press, 2006), chap.5.

38. Jane Perlez, "As Diplomacy Loses Luster, Stars Flee State Department," *New York Times,* September 5, 2000; Sanger, "Economic Engine for Foreign Policy."

39. U.S. Southern Command, "Command Strategy 2016," August 2007 (www.south com.mil/AppsSC/files/OUIO/1177092386.pdf [June 2008]).

40. George Withers and others, "Ready, Aim, Foreign Policy," Latin America Working Group Education Fund, March 2008 (www.lawg.org/docs/readyaimfp.pdf [June 2008]).

41. Thomas A. Schweich, "The Pentagon Is Muscling in Everywhere," *Washington Post,* December 18, 2008.

42. George F. Kennan, *Memoirs: 1925–1950* (Boston: Little, Brown, 1967), p. 467.

43. Bruce Jentleson and Andrew Bennett, "Policy Planning: Oxymoron or *Sine Qua Non* for U.S. Foreign Policy?" in *Good Judgment on Foreign* Policy, edited by Deborah Larson and Stanley Renshon (Lanham, Md.: Rowman & Littlefield, 2003).

44. Lucian Pugliaresi and Diane T. Berliner, "Policy Analysis at the Department of State: The Policy Planning Staff," *Journal of Policy Analysis and Management* 8 (Summer 1989): 379–94.

45. Ibid., p. 391.

46. Even when the institutional and interpersonal conditions for success are not present, policy planning can still play a useful function. Several staffers on George W. Bush's policy planning staff suggested that their most significant accomplishments were in vetoing counterproductive policies that, thankfully, never saw the light of day.

47. Kennan, *Memoirs: 1925–1950,* pp. 467–68. While Kennan was famous for loathing his days as director of policy planning, he was the exception, not the rule. Walt Rostow—S/P director under John F. Kennedy—described his experience as "the nicest job a man ever had." See David Aikman, "Those Who Thought Ahead," *Time,* May 25, 1987.

48. See also John W. Kingdon: *Agendas, Alternatives, and Public Policies,* 2nd ed. (Boston: Addison-Wesley, 1995).

Grand Strategy and Policy Planning

RICHARD N. HAASS

2

Planning for Policy Planning

The State Department's policy planning staff was launched just over sixty years ago, in May 1947. George Kennan was its first director. In many ways and with all due respect to more recent directors, it has been downhill ever since. There is one possible exception, Paul Nitze, who was Kennan's immediate successor and the principal architect of NSC-68, which in many ways translated containment into an operational national security strategy for the cold war.[1] Secretary of State George Marshall, who led the State Department when the staff was founded, gave Kennan an injunction that was as concise as it was cryptic: "Avoid trivia." Fortunately, the next secretary of state, Dean Acheson, expanded on the guidance for the policy planning staff. As Acheson wrote in *Present at the Creation,* "The general [Marshall] conceived the function of this group as being to look ahead, not into the distant future, but beyond the vision of the operating officers caught in the smoke and crises of current battle; far enough ahead to see the emerging form of things to come and outline what should be done to meet or anticipate them."[2]

Despite this advice, George Kennan left the State Department unhappy after his tenure as director of policy planning. He expressed a sense that he had come up short, that policy planning could not be made to work because there was a disconnect between it and the operational activities of the department. He wrote in his memoirs that the reason for this failure "seems to lie largely in the impossibility of having the planning function performed outside of the line of command. The formulation of policy is the guts of the work of the department, and none of it can successfully be placed outside the hierarchy which governs operations."[3] This is a real and enduring challenge to the policy planning process.

All the people who have held the job of director of policy planning since Kennan probably have had mixed feelings as well. In my experience there were elements of both frustration and satisfaction in the job. I came away feeling that I had done some things that were useful, but also wished I had been able to do more.

It is a difficult job to get right. When I taught at the Kennedy School of Government, I used to tell students that if they remembered only one thing about foreign policy, it should be that it is hard. Foreign policy is hard intellectually, given the choices and trade-offs it requires, and it is hard operationally to get anything done. Many believe that policy design is the most important element, but while design is necessary, it is far from sufficient. Policy implementation is the true test of success. This poses a challenge for policy planning because planners have tremendous advantages on policy design but tremendous disadvantages when it comes to marketing their ideas, steering them through organizations and bureaucracies, and ultimately having them emerge as "policy."

Acheson's observation captures another challenge: proximity to policymaking. If policy planners are too close to the policymaking process, there is the question of what added advantages they bring. There are already thousands of people around an administration whose job is to make and carry out policy every day. On the other hand, if policy planners are too far removed, their ability to influence operations within the government becomes modest. They must find a position close enough to have an impact but distant enough to have perspective and an ability to connect the immediate with something larger. Again, Acheson said it well: "Distraction lurks on two sides: on one, to be lured into operations; on the other, into encyclopedism."[4]

As Kennan noted, the head of policy planning does not have an operational role in government, and at the end of the day government is an operational enterprise. It is not a university. The purpose of government is to make and carry out policy. At the morning staff meeting with the secretary of state, everyone else has a specific set of operational responsibilities, but those of the director of policy planning are relatively narrow, if they exist at all. Related to this is the fact that the director is not a formal participant in the interagency process, unlike assistant secretaries with geographic and functional portfolios. Then there are under secretaries and the deputy secretary, who attend the Deputies Committee meetings. Finally there is the secretary of state, who attends meetings at the principals' level or goes to formal National Security Council meetings with the president. Unless the director is asked to accompany one of these officials to a meeting, he or she does not usually represent the State Department in the interagency arena, which is where most policies are debated and ultimately decided.

On top of these two challenges—finding the appropriate distance from the immediate policymaking process and exercising influence without an official operational role—policy planners face other hurdles. One involves the policy planning director's boss: not every secretary of state makes equal use of the policy planning staff. Not every secretary sees policy planning in the same way or values different dimensions of the job equally. Again, because the director is not an interagency official in the formal sense, much of what the director and his or her staff can accomplish depends on their principal consumer or constituent, the secretary of state. Their influence is determined in large part by the secretary, either directly or through messages he or she sends to the rest of the State Department. A good deal of policy planners' success therefore depends on the relationship between the director and the secretary, and on the secretary's temperament and receptivity to the kinds of things that policy planning produces.

A fourth challenge is timing, in two senses of the word. First, not every moment in history lends itself equally to policy planning. In the era of policy planning—that is, over the past six decades—some moments have been especially propitious because history demanded new ideas. Crises and major events came along that called for innovative responses, and there was a search for new paradigms. The September 11 attacks are a good example. After the attacks, policymakers were suddenly in the market for certain types of policies and ideas that would have received little or no support before, if they had even existed. Ends of great wars are another example. It is no coincidence that policy planning was conceived when it was, at the end of World War II. One geopolitical era had come to an end and a new geopolitical era was dawning. There was the threat of what ultimately became known as the cold war, which was more apparent to some than to others. But it was a period of trying to reshape the international order. It was a golden era for policy planning. Kennan was an extraordinary man, but it was also an extraordinary moment that lent itself to what he and his policy planning staff were seeking to do. By contrast, in the 1960s and 1970s, most of the thinking in American foreign policy was contained within a paradigm—containment—in the context of the cold war. This was not a time for producing new paradigms, but for operating within an existing one at a refined and defined level. It was not as glorious a moment for policy planning as others.

The other challenge involving timing pertains to timing within an administration. I had the advantage in principle of serving at the beginning of an administration. All things being equal, policy planners have a structural advantage at such times because all new administrations feel a certain pressure to invent. Further along in any administration new ideas gain less traction because, with the passage of time, policymakers inherit existing policies. Absent intervening events that create windows for rethinking, changing policies in an administration tends to be like steering a supertanker: difficult, slow, and sure to meet resistance.

The Obama administration's policy planners inhabit a world much different from that of Kennan and Nitze, and even from that in which President George W. Bush took office. It is important to consider the setting in which policy planning today is occurring. As I argued in "The Age of Nonpolarity," an article I wrote for the May/June 2008 issue of *Foreign Affairs*, the era of unipolarity is over. The world has gone in the past one hundred years from multipolarity in the first half of the twentieth century to bipolarity in the four decades after that to unipolarity in the two decades since the end of the cold war. We are now entering a period of nonpolarity—that is, "a world dominated not by one or two or even several states but rather by dozens of actors possessing and exercising various kinds of power." These actors include not only major powers—China, the European Union countries, India, Japan, Russia, and the United States—but also regional powers, international and regional organizations, multinational enterprises, media outlets, militias, terrorist organizations, foundations, and NGOs, among others. "Today's world is increasingly one of distributed, rather than concentrated, power."[5]

An important question for policy planners is what this means for the United States. In a nonpolar world, "the United States is and will long remain the largest single aggregation of power. . . . But the reality of American strength should not mask the relative decline of the United States' position in the world—and with this relative decline in power an absolute decline in influence and independence." The U.S. ability to act in this context is constrained. "Power and influence are less and less linked in an era of nonpolarity. U.S. calls for others to reform will tend to fall on deaf ears, U.S. assistance programs will buy less, and U.S.-led sanctions will accomplish less."[6]

This is the present, and more important the future, of the world. This will be the setting for President Barack Obama and his administration.[7] It has come about for three principal reasons. First, other states have grown better at generating and piecing together the human, financial, and technological resources that lead to productivity and prosperity. Second, the United States has accelerated and reinforced the trend toward nonpolarity through, for example, the lack of a comprehensive energy policy, the decline in its fiscal position and rise of its current account deficit, and the war in Iraq. The third reason is globalization, in which international flows of everything from drugs and weapons to manufactured goods and ideas occur with great velocity, in great volume, and more often than not outside the control of governments and without their knowledge. This weakens the influence of major powers and can strengthen nonstate actors, both benign and malign, who engage in or profit from cross-border transactions. More than anything else, nonpolarity will constitute the strategic or conceptual setting of policy planning for the foreseeable future.

Today's policy planners also face a gap between the cardinal challenges of this era, which are essentially manifestations of globalization—proliferation, terrorism, protectionism, climate change, and pandemic disease, for example—and global arrangements to meet them. The challenges are clearer than the required international responses. In some cases there is a degree of consensus on policy, but the relevant institutions do not reflect it; in other cases there is no consensus at all. The world is probably most integrated in the trade realm, but even there integration is not complete, and in other realms it is far less advanced.

Finally, there is no U.S. foreign policy doctrine that has taken the place of containment. This is still the "post–cold war era," a period referred to by a name from the past. The United States has no overall strategy to confront the threats, and take advantage of the opportunities, that are more numerous and complex today than they were during the cold war. The current era, and a doctrine to guide U.S. foreign policy in it, remains undefined.

Many ideas for such a guiding doctrine have been proposed. In *The Opportunity*, I advanced the concept of "integration." Under this doctrine, "the priority for American foreign policy should be to integrate other states into American-sponsored or American-supported efforts to deal with the challenges of globalization." On the basis of cooperative relations among the major powers, a sort of modern-day concert, a doctrine of integration would seek to build effective arrangements and promote common actions to tackle the principal global challenges. Such a policy would also, as I wrote, "work to bring in other countries, organizations, and peoples so that they come to enjoy the benefits of physical security, economic opportunity, and political freedom." [8] Despite my best efforts to promote the idea of integration, however, no guiding doctrine for post–cold war U.S. foreign policy has been embraced—although I continue to believe that integration or something close to it will gain increased support.

On top of these three general points, a daunting in-box of challenges—global, regional, economic, military, and diplomatic—faces the Obama administration. Iraq will not dominate U.S. foreign policy to the extent that it did during the Bush years, but its future remains uncertain and the need for U.S. involvement considerable. In addition, there is the war in Afghanistan or, increasingly, Afghanistan/Pakistan; nuclear weapons in North Korea; and the probability that sometime in the first years of the new administration Iran will arrive at or cross one or more nuclear thresholds. The international trade agenda is languishing. Greenhouse gas emissions are rising, with their ultimate specific effects on the Earth's climate unknown but almost certainly adverse. The United States is militarily stretched, and anti-Americanism is fairly pervasive. Barack Obama took office with the United States in a recession that is proving deep and enduring as the financial crisis has spread to the real economy. U.S. levels of oil consumption and imports remain high. The future strength and role of the dollar are uncertain. All of this adds up to a structurally demanding international system at a time when the U.S. ability to deal with it is relatively weak. President Obama will realize quickly that more of the same is not the answer. He will also realize that there is a mismatch between the challenges and commitments on one hand and the resources, particularly military, on the other. In this context, if President Obama were to continue on the course of U.S. foreign policy followed by the Bush administration much of the time, he would risk squandering a still-considerable opportunity to build a significant degree of world order. This presents an important opening to policy planners because it is likely to increase the receptiveness of the new administration to their ideas.

The president and those who work in the administration face several specific challenges. One is Iran. Since the two options of living with an Iranian nuclear weapon and using force to prevent Iran from acquiring a weapon or near-nuclear capability are so unattractive, one priority should be to put forward a diplomatic package that could be presented to the Iranian government. This package should enjoy significant international support and contain more robust carrots and sticks than those used in previous diplomatic exchanges. It should include a provision for direct talks between the United States and Iran—and delete the requirement that Iran cease all enrichment activity as a precondition for negotiations. One of the tasks for policy planners should be to help devise such a package. They should also help think through the two alternatives—using force or living with an Iranian nuclear weapon or near-nuclear capability—in case the package should not prove salable in Tehran.[9]

Second, terrorism remains an important concern, and we cannot be sure when the next major terrorist attack in the United States will occur. Much activity is already taking place within the U.S. government on how to stop terrorists who have already made their career choice—that is, how to use intelligence and law enforcement to prevent determined terrorists from carrying out attacks. There is much less work on how to dissuade people from making that career choice in the first place—that is, how to interrupt terrorists' recruiting chains. This is something I worked on a good deal when I was in policy planning. Needless to say, I did not succeed totally, but this is fertile ground for policy planners.

Climate change is another rich area. President Obama has signaled a willingness to craft policy that is significantly more ambitious than that of the Bush administration. Devising an approach is not limited to a global post-Kyoto framework; such a comprehensive accord among such a large number of countries may not prove feasible. There are also two possible variants: arrangements that deal with specific segments of the climate change problem, such as a regime that aims to limit deforestation in the tropics; and arrangements that encompass certain countries, such as an agreement to cut emissions among major industrial powers. These are issues on which fresh thinking from policy planners is warranted.

Many other items will also occupy prominent places on the Obama administration's agenda: Iraq, Afghanistan/Pakistan, North Korea, Syria, and the Israeli-Palestinian conflict, to name just a few. There is no shortage of areas that lend themselves to substantial rethinking, and the new administration may well be responsive. However, policy planners should not let such urgent items crowd out the structural. It may be easier to focus on specific issues than on structural questions involving the international system and the role of the United States in it. But these questions are highly important. They require thinking about how best to integrate the major powers into international arrangements to tackle global challenges. Russian integration is likely to pose a particular challenge, given the desirability of gaining its cooperation at the same time the United States must contend with Russia's new assertiveness and U.S. commitments to other policies, including NATO enlargement.

I referred earlier to the gap between the global challenges that define this era and global arrangements to deal with them. A textbook challenge—better yet, opportunity—for policy planners is to suggest how this gap can be closed. The realms of trade, investment, climate change, disease, nuclear nonproliferation, terrorism, and genocide are examples of where new institutions are needed or where existing institutions need to be adapted.

The advent of nonpolarity complicates but in no way reduces the need for integration. More actors require harnessing. Any global effort to meet the challenges of disease, to take one example, requires the participation not only of numerous governments but also regional and global organizations, pharmaceutical companies, foundations, and a host of nongovernmental organizations. At the same time, more actors are in a position to block or undermine collective efforts. Iran's newfound power is a reflection of nonpolarity, as is Russia's ability to dilute U.S. and European efforts designed to pressure Iran to give up an independent enrichment program. None of this is an argument against integration—there is no attractive or viable alternative in an era of global challenges and distributed power—but it is a reminder that integration will require sustained diplomatic effort led by the United States if it is to come about. There is no invisible hand ensuring order in the geopolitical marketplace.

There are as well real questions about how the United States can balance its interests in trying to affect the external behavior of countries and trying to influence their internal nature. One of the intellectual debates the Obama administration should resolve is that between a more traditionally realist foreign policy, which would focus on the foreign policies of other states, and a more idealist foreign policy, which, in the tradition of Woodrow Wilson and to a large degree George W. Bush, would concern itself more with other countries' domestic characteristics. The policy planning staff should weigh in on this debate.

All of these issues, both specific and structural, are important, and there will be many others as well. But in addition to designing new policies, policy planners must also be concerned with implementation. There are several things the policy planning staff can do to increase the chance that its ideas will be adopted as policy.

First, the secretary of state should carefully consider whom he or she appoints as director of the staff. The best people for the position tend to be scholar-practitioners. People who have a background in think tanks or universities as well as government experience do particularly well. Of course there are exceptions, for better and for worse, but this is the general rule. Moreover, if global issues are among the most important for policy planners for the foreseeable future, a director who possesses experience thinking about these issues and about how to institutionalize international responses to them is especially appropriate.

Second, it is important that policy planners limit their work to policy planning and avoid policy predicting. That is the intelligence community's role.

Policy planners should focus on their comparative advantage, which is designing policy, not divining the future.

Third, writing speeches for the secretary of state is normally part of the policy planning staff's work, and this function is important to the staff's influence. (I say "normally" as this function was transferred under Warren Christopher to the Bureau of Public Affairs.) Speeches are a valuable way to build internal support in the State Department and around the government for policy ideas. They can become important events in forcing policy questions to a decision, and they can also generate national and international support outside the bureaucracy. Speeches are, therefore, a potentially powerful instrument for policy planners.

In addition to this, it is important for the director of policy planning in particular to work well with other State Department officials. There may be a tendency to view assistant secretaries as competitors, but they can also be partners. When disagreements arise, the director of policy planning should not change his or her position for the sake of cooperation. But many things can be done jointly. It is also important that the director meet regularly with the secretary of state and other department principals. Though there is often a formal counselor at the State Department, the head of policy planning is also a counselor, and he or she should perform that function for the secretary. Another important area of work is strategy, particularly when senior officials are deciding on the department's priorities. Those with operational responsibilities in the department tend to be concerned with relatively narrow issues. Policy planners have a tremendous comparative advantage: the ability to work on every issue. Therefore, the director of policy planning can make useful contributions to discussions about priorities and how the department's areas of work fit together. This does, however, require the director to be in the room with the secretary of state and others.

The director should also try to forge an informal interagency role. Whether the director is invited to interagency meetings depends largely on others. But nothing prevents him or her from meeting regularly with people from the State Department and other agencies—such as the Defense Department, the Treasury Department, and the National Security Council—who have an official interagency role. I tried to do so often. It is useful to see officials outside the State Department because it enables policy planners to introduce ideas into the interagency process and to gauge the position of others on various issues, which helps determine how best to influence policymaking.

On a related topic, another advantage of policy planning is the ability to meet regularly with outsiders more generally, such as experts at think tanks and scholars in academia. This is an important way to hear new ideas. It was one of the activities I often engaged in as director of the policy planning staff for the secretary of state. Outside consultations can also constitute a reality check by providing a good sense of how the intellectual and political market-place is reacting to the products and ideas of policy planners.

A final important consideration is involvement in significant interagency products. Two are particularly relevant: the National Security Strategy and presidential speeches. When I was director of policy planning, one of my colleagues (Andrew Erdmann) and I succeeded in gaining influence over the first draft of the George W. Bush administration's first National Security Strategy. (Unfortunately, we had little influence over the final draft, but that is a tale best left for another day.)[10] The development of these strategies is something in which policy planners should be centrally involved. The same is true of presidential speeches. Speechwriting tends to be the messiest of all processes within the government, but the director of policy planning is the natural assistant to the secretary of state in working with the White House on presidential foreign policy speeches. These speeches offer the chance to broadcast ideas to a global audience and so are important occasions for policy planners to exercise influence.

Given all this, is policy planning possible at the present moment? The short answer is yes. Indeed, the arrival of a new administration in the current international environment is a good time for policy planning. But it is not only that. It is actually a necessary time. If I were writing *The Opportunity* today, I do not know if I would use that title. The title of any book would probably contain the word "squander" given the reality that the prospects for building international order are not as bright as they were. The year 2009 is not only the sixty-second anniversary of the creation of the policy planning staff, but also the twentieth anniversary of the end of the cold war and the fall of the Berlin Wall. In my view, historians will not judge the United States well for how it used those twenty years. The United States has not done nearly as much as it could and should have done to translate the extraordinary opportunity afforded by its absolute and relative strength into creating enduring, effective institutions to meet the global challenges of this era. If there were ever a definition of the comparative advantage of policy planners, it is this: they have the opportunity to think hard about international challenges and what must be done to meet them, and then to devise policies and build consensus within the U.S. government to do just that.

Finally, policy planning is particularly appropriate and useful for the Obama administration. The administration is seeking to differentiate itself from its predecessor in certain ways, just as all administrations do. But in addition, as noted above, the United States is extraordinarily stretched militarily and economically. The principal tool that President Obama has at his discretion is therefore the diplomatic one. Diplomacy is the area in which the United States holds its largest reserve of potential power and influence. This redounds to the advantage of policy planning. Policy planners do not control military forces and do not print money, but they can produce and disseminate ideas and seek to convince others in the U.S. government of their wisdom and utility. Given the nature of the international system and the position of the United States, there is likely to be a good case for diplomatic initiatives during the Obama presidency. The policy planning staff will face an array of problems and challenges, both those inherent in their work and those that stem from the current domestic and international environment. The items on their agenda will be both particular and structural. But despite daunting challenges—indeed, partly because of them—the coming years should be, if not quite a golden era, at least a good one for policy planning.

Notes

Adapted from the keynote address at the Conference on the Past, Present, and Future of Policy Planning, The Fletcher School, Tufts University, April 17, 2008.

1. National Security Council Report 68 was signed by President Truman on September 30, 1950.

2. Dean Acheson, *Present at the Creation* (New York: W. W. Norton, 1969), p. 214.

3. George F. Kennan, *Memoirs: 1925–1950* (Boston: Little, Brown, 1967), p. 467.

4. Acheson, *Present at the Creation*, p. 214.

5. Richard N. Haass, "The Age of Nonpolarity," *Foreign Affairs* 87 (May/June 2008): 44–56.

6. Ibid.

7. For other portraits of the world we are entering, see Andrew J. Bacevich, *The Limits of Power: The End of American Exceptionalism* (New York: Metropolitan Books, 2008); Robert Kagan, *The Return of History and the End of Dreams* (New York: Alfred A. Knopf, 2008); and Fareed Zakaria, *The Post-American World* (New York: W. W. Norton, 2008).

8. Richard N. Haass, *The Opportunity* (New York: Public Affairs, 2005), pp. 23–24.

9. For a survey of U.S. policy options toward Iran, see James N. Miller, Christine Parthemore, and Kurt M. Campbell, eds., *Iran: Assessing U.S. Strategic Options* (Washington: Center for a New American Security, 2008).

10. This is discussed in Richard N. Haass, *War of Necessity, War of Choice: A Memoir of Two Iraq Wars* (New York: Simon & Schuster, 2009).

DAVID F. GORDON *and* DANIEL TWINING

3

A Road Map for American Leadership in a Changing World

George Kennan is fondly remembered as the personification of policy planning at the dawn of America's global age. We spend less time dwelling on the fact that his organizing concept for American management of the post–World War II world was rejected.

In his Long Telegram, Kennan proposed a limited form of political containment of the Soviet Union, focused on countering its influence in times and places of our choosing—a patient and peaceful effort that would ultimately mellow Soviet power by exposing its internal contradictions. But this view was decisively repudiated by NSC-68, the guiding document of American foreign policy through much of the Cold War.[1]

NSC-68 advocated a militarized and globalized form of containment. It employed highly alarmist language about the existential threat Soviet power posed to the American way of life—in contrast to Kennan's cool and measured appraisal of the limits of Soviet strength.[2] What was Kennan's judgment of NSC-68? "I think this was a very serious and inexcusable error of policy, of thinking, on the part of people in our government. For goodness sake, at that time Russia was a ruined country. . . . They were in no position to fight a new war, nor did they want to." Kennan attacked those who "distorted" his idea by pursuing it "exclusively as a military concept," which he blamed, "*as much as any other cause,*" for leading to the "40 years of unnecessary, fearfully expensive and disoriented process of the Cold War."[3] George Kennan, the founding father of policy planning, may thus aptly be remembered for losing the argument on containment as well as for being its intellectual author.

Kennan's brilliance—and the fate of his concept—means that all of us who follow in his footsteps need to do so with a special degree of humility.

At the dawn of the cold war he was right in identifying key future trends—the link between the character of the Soviet state and its external behavior, the nature of its challenge to American power and values, the superiority of the American way of life, and the inherent contradictions of the Soviet regime that would, over time and properly managed, lead to the mellowing of Soviet totalitarianism and the collapse of the Soviet empire. But Kennan faced the same challenge that all of his successors in policy planning have grappled with: the dual requirement to identify future trends and to shape policies to exploit them.

The challenges we face today are more diffuse and, in a very real sense, will require as dexterous a diplomacy and as effective an employment of all elements of national power as did the cold war confrontation. The presidential administration of Barack Obama has its work cut out for it. But with wise leadership, sound policies, and a sustained public commitment to internationalism, we are confident, as Kennan was in his time, that the United States will rise to the challenges of the emerging international system.

The State Department policy planning staff plays a unique role during presidential transitions. It produces reports for the incoming team on the strategic landscape they will face, with suggestions for how to organize policy to meet the challenges and opportunities it presents. Although every bureau at State produces transition papers, these tend to be updates of existing policies and initiatives. Policy planning transition papers, on the other hand, are meant to provide a more strategic look at the kind of world the new administration will face, and the kinds of tools the United States has at its disposal for managing them.

This chapter provides a brief *tour d'horizon* for the Obama administration focused on three central strategic challenges for the United States. We argue that the United States can sustain its preeminent position as, in Madeleine Albright's famous phrase, the international system's "indispensable nation" over the course of the next decade and well beyond it. We challenge the emerging narrative about the inexorable erosion of American power in what is, in some ways, an increasingly multipolar world.[4] We maintain instead that its unique strengths and capabilities position the United States for enduring leadership of a twenty-first-century international order that embodies values and interests embraced by a vast part of the world.

Looking ahead, we expect American power and influence to be buffeted by three key long-term challenges: misgovernance and violent extremism in the Middle East, the rise of Asia, and the economic and information revolutions of globalization. However, the United States will remain indispensable to international security, the world economy, and the management of relations among the great and lesser powers. There will be challengers. But there is no peer competitor that can replicate this nation's global position, its strengths as a society, or its leadership. The greatest risks arise less from the emergence of new powers and more from their propensity to free-ride: the inability or unwillingness of resurgent states to carry their weight in global governance and the provision of international public goods, for which the international system remains disproportionately dependent on the United States.

The Challenges of the Greater Middle East

The broader Middle East—the region stretching from North Africa to Pakistan—is the center of the primary strategic challenge facing the United States today. It is the locus of the main struggle of our time, a struggle between violent Islamic extremists and the United States, its allies, and its partners. By spreading instability inside and outside the broader Middle East, violent extremists and those supporting them have the potential to significantly damage not only vital American interests but the international system itself. The region is characterized by ineffective governance, which creates an underlying vulnerability to extremism and complicates our ability to work with regional allies to defeat our shared adversaries. We face two distinct threats: that posed by Al Qaeda and its ideological adherents, who seek to expel U.S. and Western influences and overthrow apostate regimes in the Muslim world; and that posed by Iran, which—with the support of its allies and proxies—seeks to expand its hegemonic influence and to counter strategic objectives shared by the United States and most nations throughout the region.

Prevailing in the long-term struggle against violent extremism will require a sustained effort on several levels. Our goal is a broader Middle East that is peaceful, stable, tolerant, free of proliferation, and comprised of increasingly free and open societies better able to meet their responsibilities to their people and the wider world. This means working with friendly governments to build open societies in which economic opportunity offers surer rewards than signing up to be a suicide bomber, and in which an enlarged political space for participation and expression diminishes the incentives for, and rewards of, violent insurgency. Although the United States has made mistakes and results in Afghanistan have been mixed, there has been significant progress in Iraq. Based on lessons learned in Iraq, the United States has, in Afghanistan's unique conditions, a counterinsurgency doctrine that fuses the tools of war with the instruments of peace to shape a long-term future for countries whose democratic development is a vital national security interest of the United States.

With U.S. support, Iraq has made considerable progress toward becoming a state whose government answers to its citizens, controls its territory, creates an economic climate for investment and growth, and does not threaten its neighbors. The U.S. military surge has produced real and sustainable results. Equally significant, both Sunni and Shi'a extremists overplayed their hands, and Iraqi leaders have demonstrated a welcome determination to reassert the sovereignty of the Iraqi government over its territory, symbolized by Iraqi operations in Basra, Sadr City, and Mosul in 2008. The United States has a compelling interest in being, and being seen by the Iraqi government and people to be, an ally in the reassertion of Iraqi sovereignty. Iraq's military and political progress is already transforming the way Iraq is governed, and if sustained it has the potential to transform the strategic future of the country and the region in ways critics of the war in Iraq may have been too quick to dismiss.

The challenges the United States faces in Afghanistan do not stem primarily from a popular enemy with a compelling ideology. Whenever the Afghan people have had an opportunity to choose a course for their nation, they have voted overwhelmingly, and often at great personal risk and sacrifice, for a future of democracy, law, prosperity, and modernity, not for the medieval and antidevelopmental despotism of the Taliban. The Taliban's theory of victory is not to prevail on the battlefield or to win Afghan hearts and minds. It is to undermine the elected Afghan government, fracture the international coalition, and outlast the United States in Afghanistan. The Taliban can only prevail if the international community and our Afghan partners lose the commitment and will of the United States to help the Afghan people build their new nation. This is the hard work of a generation, not a single administration.

Together, Afghanistan and its international partners, including the United States, can render the Taliban obsolete by supporting an effective, accountable Afghan state that can provide for human security through good governance, the rule of law, and economic opportunity. Where the government and its armed forces, working with our international partners, have been able to do so—for instance in northern and eastern Afghanistan—the Taliban is in retreat. However, we have made insufficient progress in other parts of the country.

The path to victory will require putting security first and building capacity at all levels of Afghan governance. Specifically, working with our Afghan and international partners, the United States must implement a comprehensive counterinsurgency strategy, prioritize and program our resources to support that aim, empower the Afghans to enhance their security capabilities, strengthen Afghan local and provincial governance, and organize more effectively at home and in the field. Only the Afghans can build and sustain a modern nation-state; the U.S. strategy must empower them with the security environment and the capacity they need at all levels of government to realize this vision.

Pakistan's trajectory may be most important to the future of its region. It is the ultimate swing state in the campaign against extremism. Failure there would be particularly dangerous. It is essential that we coordinate our assistance, diplomatic, and security strategies to take into account the links between Afghanistan and Pakistan, neither of which can be treated in isolation, and both of which will only enjoy lasting stability through regional solutions to common challenges of governance, militancy, and underdevelopment.

History will judge the Pakistani electorate's rejection of extremism at the ballot box in February 2008 as a significant victory in the campaign against terrorism. The United States has an abiding interest in helping Pakistan to succeed in becoming a secure and prosperous democratic partner in this struggle. We face near-term challenges from the Pakistani government's unwillingness or inability to roll back terrorist sanctuaries in the tribal regions, and from the autonomy Pakistan's military/intelligence complex continues to enjoy within the Pakistani state, enabling elements of it to support Lashkar-e-Taiba, the Taliban, and other extremist groups in ways that undermine regional security and the integrity of Pakistan itself. Our long-term interest calls for partnership with Pakistan's civilian leaders to progressively shift the civilian-military balance in Pakistani politics in the direction of the former, enabling the construction of a functioning state, with institutionalized lines of command, capable of co-opting or defeating its internal adversaries.

This objective requires supporting Pakistan's democratic institutions and civil society groups with their own interest in taking on violent extremism. It requires a long-term partnership with the Pakistani government in a broad effort to promote the key elements necessary to Pakistan's long-term stability, including structural economic reforms to lay a sustainable foundation for economic opportunity, as well as investments in education, good governance, and rule of law—including in the tribal regions where the absence of governance enables terrorists to find sanctuary. We must expand programs to train the Frontier Corps to police the tribal badlands, train the Pakistani army to conduct effective counterinsurgency operations, construct border-monitoring stations, and foster political and economic development in the frontier regions. The United States has a vital interest in helping Pakistan protect and defend its democracy against extremists whose political ideology cannot prevail under accountable and effective governance.

It is a measure of our success in Iraq—the neutralization of the threat Iraq posed to its neighbors under the Saddam Hussein regime, and the extension of the writ of the elected Iraqi government across most of its territory—that Iran now looms as the primary challenger to American power in the Middle East. Iran is a revisionist state. It poses three key challenges to the United States: its quest for regional hegemony, its determination to acquire nuclear weapons capabilities, and its expressed threat to Israel's existence.

Iran's challenge is formidable. It is the world's leading state sponsor of terror, providing large caches of arms and hundreds of millions of dollars to extremist groups across the region, including in Lebanon, Palestine, Iraq, and Afghanistan. With its vast oil and gas reserves, it possesses significant energy resources. It has a large military apparatus, including a strong naval presence in the Persian Gulf and increasingly longer-range ballistic missile capabilities. And, notwithstanding a series of UN Security Council sanctions resolutions, it continues to make progress toward the development of nuclear weapons. Nevertheless, there are significant limitations to Iranian pretensions to regional dominance.

Despite its size, Iran's strategic military capabilities are limited: most of its armed forces are poorly trained, and its air force is in shambles. Mutual Sunni-Shi'a and Persian-Arab animosities serve as brakes on Iran's ability to project regional influence, provided the United States is present to give regional states alliance options not to succumb to pressure from Tehran. Iran has few strong ties in the region; the state-to-state relationships it does have are based largely on subtle and not-so-subtle intimidation, as evidenced by the often contradictory public and private statements of nearly all of Iran's neighbors. Even after years of high oil prices, the Iranian people continue to suffer from widespread unemployment, high inflation, and increasing poverty, thanks to the regime's continued mismanagement of the Iranian economy.

Finally, Iranian society is deeply divided, and Iran is not predestined to remain an authoritarian state, given its competing political traditions of limited democracy and some form of autocracy. Iranian politics has undergone several dramatic shifts over the past century, and even within the political framework of the Islamic Republic over the past thirty years. There are considerable divisions within the political class today, making it increasingly likely that change will come. However, Iranian politics remains opaque, which makes Iranian intentions hard to judge, and which in turn makes Iran's potential acquisition of nuclear weapons more dangerous.

An Iranian nuclear weapons capability could spark nuclear proliferation throughout the Middle East, embolden extremist groups, and destabilize states such as Saudi Arabia and others in the region. The goal of American statecraft, in concert with our allies, must be to prevent Iran from crossing that threshold.

Beyond that, the United States should, with skillful diplomacy backed by a strong regional security posture, be able to counter Iran's influence and constrain its regional ambitions until internal political change within Iran mellows the danger it poses to its neighbors and its region.

Overall, it is too soon to measure the success of the long U.S. campaign to transform the way the broader Middle East is governed—and the nature of the security threat its regimes, many of which combine brittle strength with institutional weakness, could pose to the United States and our allies in the future. But, to orient our strategic thinking about this troubled region, it is useful to think about the possibilities if the campaign ultimately succeeds.

Thinking ahead a few decades, imagine an economically integrated region encompassing a thriving, functioning Pakistan trading freely with a wealthy India alongside a stable Afghanistan enjoying deep economic ties with both states and its Central Asian neighbors; a prosperous Iraq at peace with its neighbors and immune from the violent neuroses of 20th century Arab nationalism; Israeli and Palestinian states living side by side; and an Iran under new leadership accountable to its people and serving as an economic engine for Central Asia and the Middle East. Imagine also the integration of this broader region into the world economy, beyond its primary role today as a supplier of energy, and the resulting socioeconomic change that has transformed Asia. Then compare this vision to the wreckage of Arab autocracy and terrorist sanctuary that the United States was confronted with on 9/11.

If we can succeed in the effort to bring about a more democratic, peaceful, and prosperous Middle East, we will not only defang the terrorist threat; we will build a new basis for stability in what is now the world's most dangerous region. It is hard work and there is no guarantee of success. But the United States has more allies than is often believed. In their different contexts, Afghans, Pakistanis, and Iraqis have all voted repeatedly for a future of democratic modernity, not domestic or international jihad. Iranians, if free to vote for all political candidates rather than those vetted by unelected clerics, would likely make the same choice. Majorities in Israel and Palestine support a two-state solution to their political conflict. Quiet political reform reinforced by economic growth is ongoing in parts of the Gulf, the Levant, and the Maghreb.

Just like Americans, Europeans, Latin Americans, Africans, and Asians, most Arabs, Persians, Afghans, and Pakistanis aspire to the fruits of democratic modernity, even if they do not crave its Western cultural by-products. The greatest danger is not that extremists present a more compelling political vision. It is that we and our allies tire of our commitment to promoting security and effective, humane governance in a region plagued by dysfunctional and autocratic states.

The Rise of Asia

In Asia the United States confronts a different set of challenges, one posed by the resurgence of multiple strong states rather than the pervasiveness of weak ones. Nonetheless, we are well positioned to remain a strong and influential player in helping shape this dynamic region over the long term because we possess unique advantages over any possible challenger, and because the potential preeminence of any other power is unacceptable to its neighbors.

China's rise is transforming the global order, but so is the broader rise of its region. Within as little as two decades, the world's four largest economies will all be in the Asia-Pacific.[5] Our bilateral alliances are necessary but not sufficient to protect our interests in this emerging Asia. Partnerships with new giants—such as India and Indonesia, as well as China—will be as important and will move us beyond the hub-and-spokes, asymmetric model of our cold war alliances in the direction of a qualitatively different kind of cooperation. A unified Korea would be a key swing state—and likely friendly balancer—in the strategic architecture.

The continuing centrality of the United States to the interests and ambitions of rising Asian states means that we will not be excluded from the Pacific century; we will be right in the middle of it. Indeed, we are today, and our position may actually be strengthening rather than slipping. Since 2001 the United States has improved its relations with every key regional power—Japan, China, India, South Korea, Australia, and Indonesia. The United States has better relations with the main powers of Asia than they have with each other, putting us in a unique position. And rather than losing our edge, polling shows that the United States is relatively popular in these countries—in particular, our reputation and our "soft power" are notably superior to those of China.[6] While China remains an economic magnet for its neighbors, events in 2008, including the largely hostile world reaction to China's suppression of the Tibetan uprising and the Olympic torch relay, demonstrated the limits of the attractive power of China's model of authoritarian development.

Indeed, thanks partly to uncertainty over its intentions inspired by the opaqueness of its political system, China's economic and military resurgence after two centuries of weakness inspires concern as well as admiration among neighboring states. For these nations, partnership with a benign, distant balancing power will remain attractive. As Singapore's ambassador to Washington,

Chan Heng Chee, has said, many Asian leaders prefer an "asymmetrically multipolar" regional order in which the United States is the strongest of several centers of strength, allowing smaller Asian states to preserve a regional pluralism of power by "borrow[ing] weight to balance the giants that bestride the scene."[7]

The United States is in a strong position in Asia. Beijing covets a special relationship with us, and we must utilize this opportunity to help shape its strategic aspirations. Should China seek to challenge our international leadership and the values it sustains, it would need to achieve regional hegemony first, thereby "escaping" Asia geopolitically to challenge us globally. Strong and wary neighbors—some fourteen of them—will make that rather difficult to do.

China does not appear to be a revolutionary state; it is more likely that the international system will change China than that China will change the international system. China increasingly defines some key diplomatic and economic interests in ways that align it with the U.S.-led system, pursuing positive-sum relations with its neighbors, remaining open to trade as a major stakeholder in the world economy, and acting with increasing responsibility in regional and international forums.

For now, China benefits disproportionately from the existing international system. The frameworks our countries have created to manage our differences—including the strategic economic dialogue between top finance officials, the senior dialogue between deputy foreign ministers, regular leadership summits, and cooperation in regional groups like the Six-Party Talks—have succeeded in focusing our cooperation on areas of shared interest while still leaving an opening to discuss important differences.

Over time, this kind of sustained interaction should encourage Chinese leaders to continue to define an interest in cooperation with the United States and, we hope, the other great powers, all of which look to the United States to socialize China as a responsible stakeholder and to assume the primary role of preparing against other possibilities. Indeed, skillful U.S. management of relations with China during the Bush administration earned the United States considerable diplomatic kudos across Asia.

However, even if Chinese leaders want their country to emerge as a status quo superpower, the size and scale of its displacement of existing balances may make that impossible; China's impact on the international system may simply be too great, irrespective of China's intentions. China may yet emerge as a strategic competitor to the United States. Questions remain: China's military modernization continues at an unprecedented pace and is oriented toward denying U.S. access to the region and exploiting unique U.S. vulnerabilities.

China continues to claim vast tracts of territory in India, and Beijing has not matched its willingness to resolve other land boundary disputes with its neighbors with a similar willingness to resolve competing maritime claims. Moreover, Chinese nationalism could place pressure on leaders in Beijing to assume a more provocative external posture. However, the United States is well positioned to respond to China should it assume a more aggressive regional course or challenge the values underpinning U.S. leadership of the international system. Chinese leaders understand this clearly and openly acknowledge America's staying power in the region and globally.

The United States has a unique strategic opportunity with India, which in many respects resembles America just over a century ago: it is a pluralistic democracy with a self-exceptional regard experiencing rapid economic growth and moving from regional to global power. While the long-term trend of closer partnership is clear, U.S.-India cooperation will not be easy or automatic, and we will face particular challenges in working together effectively on climate change and world trade liberalization. However, no other two countries share a convergence of interests across the political, economic, and military spectrums; if we play our cards right, our partnership will provide a democratic anchor of stability and security both regionally and in the emerging international order.

China launched economic reforms almost fifteen years before India, and economically India today remains roughly that far behind China. However, it has important long-term advantages—a younger workforce, a promising demographic profile, and a political system that can accommodate change— and is therefore probably less prone to political convulsion. India's "demographic dividend" will produce a rising working-age population at a time when China is graying dramatically; many expect the long-term trend rate of Indian economic growth to surpass China's within a decade.[8] India also has a geographic position in many ways superior to China's. It sits at the center of its own sea, with the energy resources of the Middle East and Central Asia on one side and the growing economies in Asia on the other.

India, like China, also needs to be able to "escape" its region to lead on the global stage. Unlike China, whose neighbors include a number of strong and capable states, India is surrounded by weak and failing ones. There is a role for the United States in encouraging India to use its economic magnetism and its considerable potential soft power as a thriving democracy to help transform its region into one that is prosperous, well governed, and secure. India should naturally be the engine of economic integration in South and Central Asia and has a compelling interest in overcoming political obstacles to realizing this vision. Otherwise, India's global rise risks being undercut by the problems of its region, including poor governance, terrorism, and lack of economic integration. India will also need to invest in its human capital and mobilize its people to embrace the international responsibilities that accompany great power.

Historically, Japan has shown a striking ability to rapidly transform itself in response to international conditions, as seen in the Meiji break from isolation, the rise to great power in the twentieth century, the descent into militarism, and renewal as a dynamic trading state. The conventional narrative about the rise of China and India has obscured the continued relevance of Japanese power: it has the world's second largest economy, a navy three times the size of Great Britain's, an advantageous geographic position, an enduring alliance with the United States, considerable soft power in Asia, and a propensity to reform and renew itself in the face of structural challenges from the international system.

Japan is struggling to become a "normal" power, and astute commentators recognize that it, no less than China and India, will shape Asia's strategic future.[9] We are in the singular position of having excellent relations with all three countries, and special relations with Japan and India that are growing stronger, not weaker, even as these democracies expand their military capabilities and look to the United States to help them secure membership in international great-power clubs like the UN Security Council.

New institutions will also define Asia's emerging strategic landscape. Fears of an insular Asian economic and political bloc are overblown: most Asian states prefer a form of open regionalism that includes the United States and friendly powers like India and Australia. New institutions could include a free-trade area of the Pacific tying together the world's most dynamic economies. They could include a formalized Asian great-power concert, for which the Six-Party Talks have laid a foundation. We will also see new partnerships among Asian democracies, whether in the form of a U.S.-Japanese-Indian-Australian quadrilateral, the U.S.-Japan-Australia and U.S.-Japan-Korea trilaterals, more formalized alliances linking militarily capable Asian democracies with NATO partners, or a broader grouping of democracies dedicated to promoting good governance under the emerging Asia-Pacific Democracy Partnership.

Finally, Asia's political transformation—the regionwide embrace of democracy—will be as important as its economic transformation in determining its strategic future, and our role in it. More people live under democratic rule in Asia today than in any other region. Vibrant U.S. relations with all of China's neighbors, and the spread of democracy across the region, will help sustain a pluralistic regional order in which norms of democracy and good governance can flourish in ways that, over time, we believe will shape China's own internal debate about political liberalization.

Competing and Thriving in a Globalized World

Just as we have indispensable roles to play in the broader Middle East and in Asia, so the United States continues to have singular advantages in an increasingly globalized world. There have been previous waves of globalization across human history, including those led by Arab traders and European imperialists.[10] The current wave of post–cold war globalization grew out of the political-economic order the United States constructed in its sphere after 1945, an order that was once limited to Western Europe and Japan but now stretches worldwide. The increasingly global character of this order is a reflection of the success of market capitalism in enabling "the rise of the rest."

The U.S. financial crisis of 2008–09 may further catalyze the diffusion of economic and financial power in the international system. But given the increasingly interdependent nature of the global economy and the vulnerability of every major economy to similar forces, it will not obviate the need for a strong U.S. role in both mitigating its impacts and forging effective partnerships to sustain global growth. Furthermore, the excesses that resulted in the need for significant public interventions do not herald the death of the free-market system. Far from being a harbinger of the kind of state-led capitalism that has arisen in other parts of the world, the global financial crisis suggests the need for better governance to preserve, strengthen, and ensure the adequate functioning of free markets. Countries with strong, responsive, and accountable institutions—like the United States—are well positioned to pursue such reforms.

This era of globalization was built on a foundation of American strategic preeminence and an Internet-based information revolution that was made in the USA. Much has been written about the erosion of American power caused by the dispersion of economic growth and technological innovation worldwide. This is largely nonsense. Consider the historical parallel of the economic recovery of Western Europe after World War II. Europe's economic reconstruction and the decades of growth that followed did not weaken the United States. European recovery and dynamism strengthened our economy and our international leadership, even as the American share of aggregate global financial and manufacturing indicators diminished over the decades following 1945.

Similarly, today, the diffusion of wealth and the dispersion of economic growth in every region is a welcome development for the United States, one that underpins our own economic dynamism in an open world economy constituted, like our own, by the wealth-generating effects of market capitalism. Other countries do not necessarily want to import our culture. But they have embraced economic openness and increasingly recognize its most important political implication—that innovation and modernity require an open society.

America will retain unique advantages in an economically and informationally globalized world. We still provide the public goods that undergird this system, and we are among its principal beneficiaries, as are China and other emerging powers. We should not underestimate our strengths: the United States has a unique capability to bring together technology, entrepreneurship, and capital in a way that no other country appears positioned to match, today or in the longer term. Moreover, almost every other major and rising power recognizes that it has a strong stake in the economic and financial health of the United States, as a source of capital and technology, as a market, as the world's leader in producing human capital through advanced education, and as a provider of the international public goods that sustain the global economy. The global financial crisis has only underscored the continued centrality of the U.S. economy to the health of the global economy.

Nonetheless, the recent financial turmoil highlights the reality that globalization is entering a new and more challenging period. While the United States remains preeminent across a broad range of power indicators, we now live in a multipolar financial world. There are globally competitive financial centers in Europe, Asia, and the Gulf, and an emergent competitor to the dollar as the world's reserve currency in the form of the euro. There are new financial actors, including sovereign wealth funds and national oil companies, that are affecting markets and the nature of global economic competition. The United States will need to embrace a series of astute policy choices to sustain the competitiveness of its financial sector in the face of these trends.

More specifically, the United States needs to be far more vigorous in its leadership on free trade and capital markets, starting at home. Trade and capital flows from overseas are a critical source of our prosperity. In good times, their benefits also have an important political effect: they hedge against foreign policy isolationism. But in periods of economic downturn, leaders must explain clearly and consistently to the American people that the temptation of domestic protectionism impoverishes, not enriches, affluent societies, as the world learned in the 1930s.

America's governing elites today are heirs to a long-standing bipartisan political tradition, going back to the time of Franklin Roosevelt and Cordell Hull, of strong American support for an open international economy as a foundational source of U.S. power and leadership. Since the end of the cold war, presidents George H. W. Bush, Bill Clinton, and George W. Bush have sustained a commitment to continued openness for the American and global economies. There is no question that the American public today is becoming more skeptical on this subject. In the future, our leaders must more aggressively shape American public opinion in favor of our vital stake in a liberal international trade and financial regime that sustains our people's prosperity and our country's preeminence.

The most recent bout of financial turbulence need not repeat the calamitous events leading to the Great Depression, which was caused as much by policy inaction as by market dynamics. A commitment by the U.S. to open markets is vital to avoid a similar spiral of economic nationalism, beggar-thy-neighbor policies in the form of the Smoot-Hawley tariff, and rising protectionism. World trade is expected to shrink in 2009 for the first time since 1982, and capital flows to developing economies are forecast to plunge by as much as 50 percent.[11] Given their dependence on global trade and capital flows, China, India, and a host of developed and developing nations alike have a tremendous stake in continuing to remove trade and capital barriers even in the midst of a recessionary environment.

The global financial crisis may provide an opportunity similar to the Bretton Woods conference of 1944 to reshape, update, and adjust the international economic architecture in a recognition that new actors and new financial instruments have fundamentally changed the landscape. This is unquestionably necessary in a world radically different from the one John Maynard Keynes and Harry Dexter White knew when they negotiated the creation of the International Monetary Fund and what became the World Bank. Today none of the world's major creditor nations are members of the G-7; questions remain about the capacity of the G-20 to serve as a new international financial steering committee, given its size and diversity of membership. A global financial crisis nonetheless places in stronger relief the need for rising actors like China, India, Saudi Arabia, and Brazil to have a greater stake in existing institutions, and new "rules of the road" appear necessary to coordinate oversight of capital markets, the interactions of central banks including but not limited to the G-7, and the monitoring of financial risk.

Long-term challenges like global warming and energy security also demand U.S. leadership. We cannot manage the global commons alone. Rising prosperity, especially in Asia, gives us new, more capable partners with whom we can tackle these issues. This will require China and India, in particular, to define their own interest in global governance. From free trade to energy security to global warming, our challenge with China and India is to vest in them shared responsibility for sustaining the global commons on which our universal livelihood depends.

Leading the growing number of competent and capable powers to tackle the world's thorniest global challenges could be even harder work than forging the cold war containment coalition, because the threats are less immediate and more diffuse, the stakes are greater than control of territory or political influence, and it is harder to organize diverse yet effective coalitions to tackle systemic challenges than to defend against a territorial threat from a defined adversary.

American leadership will be indispensable to this effort. So will be strong, committed partners. Unlike during the cold war, when one of America's principal problems was the weakness of our allies in Western Europe and Japan, in the coming decades we should benefit from the growing capacity of countries such as Japan, India, the European Union, China, Russia, and Brazil to work in concert to police and sustain the global commons.

Conclusion

Beleaguered by headlines about the inexorable rise of China, setbacks in Afghanistan, the weakness of the Pakistani state, the Iranian nuclear challenge, the continuing danger of terrorist attack, the fragility of the international financial system, and the complex threats posed by climate change, leaders in Washington might be forgiven for believing that America's moment has passed, and that the best the United States can hope for is to play defense in "someone else's century."[12]

They would be mistaken. New powers and forces are at work that erode America's relative material advantages. But the United States has a unique and, in some respects, unprecedented opportunity to lead and help shape the emerging international order in ways that advance enormous shared interests and secure our country's long-term preeminence among multiple strong states operating in a dynamic and globalized world. We will remain the international system's indispensable nation, buoyed by a uniquely strong, dynamic, and adaptable society. We cannot be complacent; but we should be confident in our capacity to manage our interests in the future we see before us.

Indeed, we should celebrate the global spread of political and economic modernity through market capitalism and good governance as a historic success for American foreign policy. With the collapse of the Soviet empire and the embrace by the world economy of billions of people in Eurasia and what used to be called the third world, the liberal international order we constructed with our Western European and Japanese allies within our shared cold war sphere has gone global. This represents the ultimate victory of our leadership and our ideals in the long twilight struggle from 1947 to 1989. History may judge the wave of globalization that followed, and the concomitant spread of our ideals, to be the greatest payoff of the West's victory in the cold war.

New forms of global governance will be essential to manage systemic economic and environmental challenges to this international order that has done greater good for a greater number of people than any previous system. Indeed, only since the end of the cold war can we speak of an international system that is truly global in scope, one that does not exclude (or treat as mere subjects) much of humankind, unlike the European great-power order, the British imperial system, and the cold war order. The scale, scope, and complexity of governance in today's international system are incapable of management by any one state, no matter how powerful, as we have seen in the systemic financial crisis of 2008–09.

With wise leadership, the United States will thrive in the emerging twenty-first-century international system. We have an indispensable and unique role to play to manage a changing Middle East, a rising Asia, and a globalized economy. Other great powers will challenge our leadership, but with sustained technological and economic dynamism at home, a continued commitment by the American people to lead internationally, smart diplomacy, and robust forward engagement, we should be able to fend off efforts to exclude us from key regions or undermine our position in the international system. Indeed, the greatest danger is not that resurgent Asian states will challenge us for leadership of the international system; nor is it that great-power revanchism of the kind Russia displayed in its illegal and ill-judged invasion of Georgia will lead us into conflicts we cannot win. The United States is well positioned to manage and prevail over any imaginable great-power adversary.

Rather, the risk is that these and other important powers, like the European Union, Brazil, and South Africa, will not assume their share of responsibility for the provision of international public goods—from sustaining the open international economy to tackling climate change and dealing with energy scarcity on an increasingly crowded planet. The greatest challenge for the United States in the coming decades is unlikely to be fending off peer competitors in zero-sum military conflicts, but vesting rising powers with responsibilities in global governance commensurate with their international clout and their status as beneficiaries of a global order sustained disproportionately by American leadership. This will be especially hard given that, in the past, new rules of global governance have been forged after major wars. The challenge today is to vest new powers with shared leadership, and develop new rules to govern the commons, in a time of peace.

In this complex and uncertain world, policy planning will be an increasingly important exercise. But if policy planning is essential, particular policy planners may not be. George Kennan's fate is instructive. Having lost the bureaucratic battle pitting his limited conception of political containment against the more muscular, militarized doctrine of global containment advocated by his rivals, Kennan was replaced as director of policy planning at the State Department by the author of the document he despised (NSC-68): Paul Nitze. The United States will remain indispensable to managing a complex world; individual policy planners will not.

Notes

1. National Security Council Report 68 was signed by President Truman on September 30, 1950.

2. See, for instance, David Campbell, *Writing Security: United States Foreign Policy and the Politics of Identity* (Manchester University Press, 1998).

3. George Kennan, interview for CNN's *Cold War: Episode I—Comrades,* May–June 1996 (www.cnn.com/SPECIALS/cold.war/episodes/01/interviews/kennan/). We are grateful to Kori Schake for drawing our attention to these remarks.

4. For three different versions of this argument, all worth reading, see Richard Haass, "The Age of Non-Polarity," *Foreign Affairs* 87 (May/June 2008): 44–56; Fareed Zakaria, *The Post-American World* (New York: W. W. Norton, 2008); and Kishore Mahbubani, *The New Asian Hemisphere* (New York: Public Affairs, 2008).

5. Those four are the United States, China, India, and Japan. Goldman Sachs, "Dreaming with BRICS: The Path to 2050," *Global Economics Weekly,* October 1, 2003 (www2.goldmansachs.com/ideas/brics/brics-dream.html [December 8, 2008]).

6. Chicago Council on Global Affairs, *Soft Power in Asia: Results of a Multinational Survey of Public Opinion,* June 2008 (www.thechicagocouncil.org/dynamic_page.php?id=75 [December 8, 2008]); Michael J. Green, "The Iraq War and Asia: Assessing the Legacy," *Washington Quarterly* 31, no. 2 (Spring 2008) (www.twq.com/08spring/docs/08spring_green.pdf [January 28, 2009]).

7. Chan Heng Chee, "China and ASEAN: A Growing Relationship," remarks delivered to the Asia Society Texas Annual Ambassador's Forum and Corporate Conference, Houston, February 3, 2006 (http://app.mfa.gov.sg/ [December 8, 2008]).

8. Tushar Poddar and Eva Yi, "India's Rising Growth Potential," Global Economics Paper no. 152 (New York: Goldman Sachs, January 22, 2007) (www2.goldman sachs.com/ideas/brics/book/BRIC-Chapter1.pdf [January 28, 2009]).

9. Bill Emmott, *Rivals: How the Power Struggle between China, India, and Japan Will Shape Our Next Decade* (New York: Harcourt, 2008); Brahma Chellaney, *Asian Juggernaut: The Rise of China, India, and Japan* (New Delhi: HarperCollins India, 2006); Kenneth Pyle, *Japan Rising: The Resurgence of Japanese Power and Purpose* (New York: Public Affairs, 2007); Richard Samuels, *Securing Japan: Tokyo's Grand Strategy and the Future of East Asia* (Cornell University Press, 2007).

10. Nayan Chanda, *Bound Together: How Traders, Preachers, Adventurers, and Warriors Shaped Globalization* (Yale University Press, 2008).

11. Mark Landler, "Dire Forecast for the Global Economy and World Trade," *International Herald Tribune*, December 10, 2008 (www.iht.com/articles/2008/12/10/business/10global.php [January 28, 2009].

12. Then–Secretary of State Condoleezza Rice aptly took on this argument, and made the case for American staying power, in Condoleezza Rice, "Remarks at the Centennial Dinner for the Economic Club of New York," New York City, June 7, 2007 (www.state.gov/secretary/rm/2007/06/86200.htm [December 8, 2008]).

JEFFREY W. LEGRO

4

A "Return to Normalcy"? The Future of America's Internationalism

When new presidents take office, expectations for change always run high. Such is the case for Barack Obama. Yet a major change in U.S. foreign policy in the next few years is unlikely in the absence of unforeseen events. The United States, after a brief experimentation with the Bush doctrine, has returned to the basic "American Internationalism" (AIM) foreign policy that guided the United States between 1946 and 2001. There remains widespread support for continuing the AIM agenda, featuring U.S. international leadership, military superiority, support for democracies abroad, free trade, and multilateralism. To be sure, there will be "Anything but Bush" tactical adaptations in policy, especially in the Middle East, and a potentially influential change in diplomatic style, but even the George W. Bush administration in its second term had already largely returned to the fold of the AIM postwar tradition. President Obama is likely to remain there, and that is mostly a good thing.

What is possible in 2009 and after, however, is growing friction between the American Internationalism view and emerging international conditions—leading to mounting pressure for change. AIM strategy will be challenged by divergences in the U.S.-European consensus on international order, mounting U.S. economic difficulties, and the rising position of countries like China and India that have different needs.

Yet what is still absent in the United States is a worldview suited to emerging conditions that has enough political support to replace AIM. Policy planning in the years ahead therefore will involve (1) implementing the neo-American Internationalism, (2) attending to failed expectations, and (3) planning for an alternative set of strategic principles. American internationalism has served the country well, but in order to meet new international problems (such as terrorism and global warming) in the face of slowly dissipating U.S. power and the erosion of post–World War II institutions, it will likely need to be significantly modified over the longer run.

In what follows I discuss why no major reformulation of foreign policy is likely in the near term, what changes we can expect, and what forces will create pressure for change over the longer term. The conclusion addresses the implications for policy planning.

The Puzzling Power of the Status Quo

Although presidential transitions would seem to be the ideal time for major changes in foreign policy, there are several reasons why the Obama administration is unlikely to reorient basic principles. First, major change in U.S. foreign policy is rare, and the conditions that favor such a change are not present. Second, the United States under George W. Bush attempted to shift its foreign policy, and the result was a return to tradition. Finally, even though there are signs of polarization in the United States, there is widespread consensus among Americans for continuity in foreign policy.[1] Support for AIM is also fairly strong abroad.

Major transitions in U.S. foreign policy—ones that affect the U.S. willingness to lead or join international institutions, develop and use its military power, engage in trade, and actively promote political change in foreign countries—are unusual. For example, since the founding in 1776, the U.S. view on how to relate to major-power politics has changed only *once*. In the midst of World War II, the United States discarded its long-standing desire to separate itself from the political-military entanglements of the European-devised system and instead chose to integrate itself, maintain and use its military power, adopt free trade, and promote democracy outside of the Americas.[2]

The common wisdom is that the United States alters its foreign policy dramatically "when it needs to," such as in response to crises, changes in the balance of power, or a perceived threat. For example, the United States did indeed shift in response to Pearl Harbor, the demands for U.S. involvement in World War II, and the conditions that quickly followed in the cold war.

Yet even in response to crisis, change is difficult; in normal times it takes extraordinary effort. Big events—wars, geopolitical shifts, depressions, revolutions, and even surprise attacks—are often cathartic moments in national politics. The problem is they are not always catalysts of change. Consider for example how Woodrow Wilson's attempt at change after World War I went down in flames despite unprecedented newfound U.S. power at the time. And all the jawing on the need for a new strategy after the cold war left not a trace, despite the disappearance of the Soviet threat.

It turns out that it is hard to alter foreign policy mind-sets that have been inspired by searing episodes in history, that are embedded in national institutions and educational systems, and that are protected by interest groups that benefit from them. Such mind-sets generate governmental capabilities and abilities that are not easily amended—as the nation found out in its effort to deal with terrorism in the run-up to 9/11.[3] It is therefore not surprising that continuity is the norm in foreign policy paradigms.[4]

Even when people can think outside the boundaries of the dominant mind-set (which they often do), those who want to challenge tradition nonetheless face significant hurdles. It can be hard for individuals to know if others desire change, and if they do, how much they will risk in acting on their preferences. Lacking such information, they cannot be sure that their own desire and efforts for change will have any effect. They must mount a case for why the old ideas are defunct, which can involve considerable effort; and because doing so threatens tradition, they invite social and political criticism.

Even when powerful political actors can agree that the old ideas must go, they still have to agree on a new set of ideas. Yet the formation and institutionalization of new ideas breeds strife and uncertainty because particular orientations offer differing costs and benefits to domestic groups, which can stalemate over which, if any, new direction is more desirable. For this reason, continuity is again a potent force.

Given these hurdles, elections are typically not occasions for major change. They do not provide the ammunition that critics need to undermine a standing orthodoxy. Consider, for example, the cold war period. Different presidents had different approaches to American Internationalism, but the basic strategy remained fairly stable throughout the period—until 2001. As the 9/11 Commission report concluded, despite changes in the world that made terrorism a threat, the United States was trapped in a cold war mentality and constrained by cold war capabilities.[5] Then, as now, elections alone are unlikely to alter that mind-set.

A second reason that change is not likely is that we have already seen one major attempt—the Bush revolution—to reorient foreign policy. The failure of that effort only strengthened the return to a neo-AIM mind-set.

In the wake of the 9/11 terrorist attacks, the United States adopted what the Yale historian John Lewis Gaddis called *potentially* "the most sweeping shift in

U.S. grand strategy since the beginning of the Cold War."[6] The Bush doctrine's "American Supremacy" view (in contrast to AIM) was a three-legged stool emphasizing unilateral action (as a rule, not the exception), the preventive use of force (rather than reactive containment), and an expanded geographic reach (that is, outside the Western hemisphere) for intervening overtly (not covertly) in the domestic affairs of other countries—including forcible regime change. None of the legs of this stool were new; each had precedents in earlier eras.[7] Yet cumulatively, especially as declared national strategy (not just tools used in unusual situations), the three legs represented a potential sea change in U.S. thinking about how to relate to the world.[8]

That effort achieved some successes but, mired in Iraq, resented by international opinion, and largely perceived as ineffective, lost significant support. In the 2008 presidential election, both the Democratic and Republican candidates promised a retreat from the Bush agenda, and a return to the AIM consensus.[9] Indeed the Bush administration itself, in 2005 and after, had already largely returned to a position that was more akin to its predecessors than that of the doctrine initiated after 9/11.[10]

So when a major shock of the type that can spark major change in strategy occurred (the 9/11 attacks), the Bush administration undertook an effort to reorient U.S. strategy according to what came to be known as the Bush doctrine; but because expectations were undermined by results, defenders of the AIM view have largely succeeded in reestablishing that foreign policy.

The third reason why a major change is unlikely in the next few years is elite and mass support for the foundational principles of AIM. In a 2008 volume that included the views of experts on U.S. foreign policy representing a range of partisan and ideological perspectives, all agreed on the desirability of U.S. leadership in world affairs, U.S preponderance in power, the spread of democracy, open trade and finance, and collaboration with other countries.[11] In short, right or left, libertarian or socialist, elite thinkers largely embrace an agenda that resembles AIM thinking.

This consensus, moreover, is not just limited to elites. Opinion polls indicate that the public supports the same principles, with some nuances:

—Americans do not want to foot the bill or be the sole leader, but 70 percent of those polled want to see the United States take an active part in world affairs—a proportion akin to that in the early 1950s and that has remained relatively steady since then.[12]

—Fifty-five percent of Americans today agree that maintaining military superiority is an important goal, and 53 percent believe the United States should retain the majority of its overseas military bases.[13]

—On free trade, the public is increasingly less enthusiastic than elites, but support for expanding openness does exist. When asked about connections between the U.S. economy and others abroad, 60 percent believe that expansion is mostly good, while 35 percent believe it is mostly bad.[14]

—On international collaboration, the majority of those polled in recent years think the United States should work more closely with allies (91 percent), consider the views and interests of other countries (90 percent), deal with problems like terrorism and the environment by working through international institutions (69 percent) and strengthen the United Nations (79 percent).[15]

Support for these principles is not limited to the United States. Perhaps surprisingly, they also receive encouragement from opinion abroad. To be sure, there are some variations—for example, fewer numbers abroad welcome U.S. military preponderance. Still, there is noteworthy international support for U.S. leadership, the spread of democracy, globalization and economic openness, and international cooperation.[16]

In sum, the difficulty of enacting major changes in foreign policy, the failed effort at transformation represented by the Bush doctrine, and the enduring considerable support at home and abroad for AIM suggest that a major change is both unlikely and undesirable in the near future.

Adaptation, not Transformation

To suggest that major changes are unlikely in U.S. foreign policy is not to rule out all changes. President Obama will certainly bring a different style of diplomacy and different approaches to particular countries, such as Iran, and issues, such as global warming. There is likely to be some movement in reaction to unpopular policies of the prior administration and to fulfill campaign pledges. Likewise there will be important disagreements over the tactics of implementing AIM that could produce notable adaptations. But for the most part these differences will be incremental and not affect the basic tenets of AIM.

A new presidency always brings some changes and alterations. In the United States large numbers of political appointees come and go, especially when there is a change of political party in the White House. George W. Bush's policies in 2000 were often described as "ABC" (Anything but Clinton) and his administration did much to try to distinguish its approach from that of its predecessor. That pattern is not unfamiliar: Reagan was anti-Carter, who was anti-Nixon, who was anti-Kennedy/Johnson, who were anti-Eisenhower, who was anti-Truman. President-elect Obama made some notable gestures to dampen anti-Bush rhetoric, but given that one of the first acts of his admin-istration was to close Guantanamo Bay, a symbol of the Bush presidency, the dynamic seems alive and well. All this "anti" sentiment in the past, of course, produced adjustments, but not the remaking of fundamental principles.[17]

A second reason to believe that we will see adaptations in 2009 and beyond is that campaign promises are a source of new initiatives. Many people believe that such promises or campaign pledges are just cheap talk that is jettisoned when the candidate reaches office. In some cases that belief has proven cor-rect—consider Eisenhower's 1952 pledge to liberate Eastern Europe and John-son's pledge in 1964 not to enlarge the U.S. presence in Vietnam.

Still, the broader evidence seems to suggest that politicians actually do a rea-sonable job of fulfilling their campaign promises. By the measure of one study, between 1912 and 1976, presidents fulfilled some 65 to 70 percent of their for-eign policy campaign promises.[18] Other studies suggest similar dynamics.[19]

Disputes over how to implement AIM are also likely to produce adapta-tions. While there may be consensus on such broad principles as leadership, military preponderance, democratization, globalization, and cooperation, how those actually get turned into policy are matters for heated discussion. For example, leaders and parties may approach them with distinct emphases. "Red state" Republicans see leadership as having more to do with authority and competence in the use of power, whereas "blue state" Democrats believe it rests in adherence to international law and respect for foundational U.S. principles such as human rights.How to pursue other broad principles will also be open to debate and variation in policy.[20] For example, many agree on the need to maintain U.S. military preponderance, but may disagree on how to do it and what to do with our capabilities. Should the United States preserve its traditional conventional battlefield emphasis or instead encourage a new counterinsurgency strategy? The spread of democracy may be widely embraced, but should it involve the use of force, a focus on electoral democ-racy, or developing responsive institutional competence in foreign countries? And although most see the need for better multilateral cooperation in the years ahead, the schemes for achieving it come in many colors. Should the United States attempt a new world concert with the European Union, Russia, and China? Or should it focus more on bringing the world's democracies together? Should it work within existing institutions or create new ones?

These are important questions, and the way they are answered will be another source of adaptation in U.S. foreign policy in the years ahead. One issue that will most influence the immediate future of U.S. foreign policy is the fate of intervention in Iraq and Afghanistan. How U.S. involvement in those countries plays out, how it is handled, and the implications that follow will importantly shape U.S. policy. Those results will again be a source of adaptation in the AIM emphasis of U.S. foreign policy (especially regarding when to intervene and where), but probably not a cause of fundamental change. Recall that Vietnam did not fundamentally alter AIM in an earlier period, though it did affect the U.S. inclination to intervene with its own military on the periphery.

The Sources of Potential Change

To say that a major transformation in U.S. foreign policy is improbable is not to say that it is impossible. In general, such changes are likely when inflated expectations for current policy are subsequently dashed by events with significant and unwanted consequences. Such circumstances undermine the defenders of tradition and allow their critics to coalesce. When that happens *and* when critics are able to coordinate on an effective alternative strategy, U.S. foreign policy is prone to change.

The two most likely triggers of major transformation in U.S. foreign policy are: (1) an unexpected shock and (2) the growing tension between AIM and the demands of emerging international politics.

Shock

The first trigger is widely recognized—that is, an unforeseen major crisis or unexpected event that forces decisionmakers to return to first principles and reorient the prior pattern of international activity. One can imagine several possibilities that might undermine AIM (though the events we cannot imagine are often the most powerful).

This could occur if another significant terrorist attack against U.S. citizens takes place, especially one on U.S. soil. If, after all the effort extended abroad in Afghanistan and Iraq, the United States still cannot prevent such attacks, any form of forward-based internationalist defense and diplomacy will face a difficult test of validity from an onslaught of critics. This is especially true if it is accompanied by continuing or heightened international criticism of the United States. After all, if U.S. efforts to help itself and the world are met by the hostility of friends and enemies alike, Americans will wonder, what is the purpose of the whole effort?

In such circumstances it is not unthinkable that the relatively marginalized anti-internationalist groups in the United States would gain new momentum. Pat Buchanan and his fellow travelers would look prescient. "Off-shore

balancing"—code words for a significant political-military withdrawal—
would look more inviting. The challenge of terrorism would no longer be
confronted abroad, but instead be met with ever more vigorous "homeland
defense" efforts, especially those focusing on immigration, border and trade
controls, and antimissile measures.

The main brake on such a strategy is the continuing economic internationalism of the United States. How could the United States shrink its perime-
ter with so many interests abroad? Such a potential shift would not involve,
at least at first, the economic internationalism that has characterized U.S. foreign policy in both the AIM and Supremacy views. Yet the question correctly
presumes a link between economic and political-military stability, and it is not
clear to what degree this interdependence is appreciated, especially by those
unfamiliar with the history of the interwar period. There are sectors of the
American public that favor a renewed economic nationalism and who would
take advantage of the same conditions to "defend American jobs"—largely by
reining in the liberal trading order developed since World War II.

Another scenario that might motivate change is closely related to this last
thought—that is, some sort of meltdown of the global economic architecture.
This of course happened before in the interwar period. Given the ongoing
financial crisis, it is once again thinkable. The rapidity with which economic
events are transmitted through the system can be alarming. The fallout from
housing market turmoil in the United States and other countries has produced a global financial meltdown and recession, and as of this writing may
still unravel into something worse. It is difficult to say how such a dramatic
event would alter U.S. foreign policy, but it could have far-reaching consequences. In the interwar period, the Depression first affected U.S. foreign eco
nomic policy (much the same as today), but through its influence on the rise
of fascist regimes and their subsequent aggression ultimately nurtured American internationalism during World War II.

As noted above, shocks and major events only destabilize foreign policy to
the extent that the strategy does not anticipate them and that they present
undesirable consequences. Not all shocks actually undermine policy. Consider again the end of the cold war, which did not contradict the expectations
of the existing U.S. approach or bring unwanted results. Thus, despite the
vastly altered international arena after 1989, with no challenge to the U.S.
orthodoxy and no negative results for critics and reform-minded strategists
to use as ammunition, there was no stirring America's transformational tendencies. The defenders of AIM easily dismissed the whining of change advocates. A series of sound-thinking commissions on terrorism and other new

threats in the 1990s were virtually ignored by the mass media and marginalized in Washington.

Plate Friction

The second and more likely source of transformation will gain momentum slowly in the years ahead. The best way to understand it is in terms of plate tectonics. Like earthquakes, which are often caused by the slow compression of massive geological formations moving against each other, in U.S. foreign policy the two plates now starting to collide are American expectations for its neo-AIM strategy and actual international conditions.

Both major party candidates in the 2008 presidential campaign argued that their foreign policies would be more successful because they would return to the prior pattern of multilateral consultation and cooperation. In short, they said that the wrongs in U.S. foreign policy could be righted by pursuing AIM foreign policy—that doing so will allow the United States to better achieve its interests. Much is expected of this correction to the supposed faults of the Bush era.

The problem is that the high expectations that are now being attached to neo-AIM thinking are likely to be frustrated by emerging conditions in the international arena. One concerns U.S. standing in the world. A legacy of the Bush administration is mistrust and diminished stature of the United States in world politics—a situation that may make U.S. efforts at collaboration in 2009 and after more difficult than they need be. It might be that President Obama's considerable popularity worldwide will ameliorate the anti-Americanism that developed in the last five years of Bush's presidency. But such sentiments are often the product of different factors, could be somewhat embedded at this point, and thus could prove slower to change. To the extent that U.S. standing is being driven by forces other than the policies or personalities of the past administration, or the attractions of the new, then the challenges could be more significant.

Another reason why neo-AIM thinking is likely to be difficult is that the international architecture of that program looks increasingly brittle. Many of the institutions at the heart of the internationalist project—the United Nations(UN), the Nuclear Non-Proliferation Treaty (NPT), the World Trade Organization (WTO)—are not working as envisioned.[21] There are ways to duct tape and refurbish them, but it seems they are less suited to the world that is ahead. Equally problematic, few new institutions have been created even when there is a clear functional need, such as combating terrorism or dealing with global warming or managing the distribution of scarce resources.

A plausible solution is to establish new institutions better suited to the twenty-first-century global arena.[22] Yet the conditions for doing so are now very different than in the wake of World War II. International order in the past has been primarily a function of deals cut among the great powers, and the collapse of order a product of their clashes.[23] Although there is still considerable support abroad for U.S. AIM thinking, the longer-term viability is being challenged by a shifting pattern of power and interests in the international arena involving the United States, Europe and Japan, and China.

The decline of contemporary order is at least in part due to a fissure between Europe and the United States on the purpose and process of global management. This divide is not about the end of transatlantic cooperation. In the scheme of things the United States and Europe continue at a relatively high level of amity. Nor is it about the end of NATO, the security pact at the heart of the Atlantic bargain. NATO still serves a shared desire to provide stability on the continent and protect from either anarchy or domination from the East. It is likely to remain intact for some time (especially with the reemergence of an assertive Russia).

Though they had significant clashes during the cold war, in recent years Europe and the United States have seemed to diverge more often, perhaps as the central issues of global politics have moved beyond the geography of the continent, and especially on basic approaches to order. As Robert Kagan has famously articulated, the Americans are from Mars and Europeans from Venus.[24] Europe has favored an international order that is based on robust multilateralism, autonomous international institutions, "rule-based" global governance, and the avoidance of the use of military force.[25] The United States in contrast has tended to favor the exercise of its dominant power through the military and in other forms. It has preferred the unilateral exercise of power where possible, and especially in recent years in bilateral deals when unilateralism doesn't work. Socioeconomically, the United States favors a more laissez-faire capitalism than the social welfare mentality on the Continent. Europe believes the authority-commingling EU model should be extended to the global level; the United States has often preferred to protect its sovereignty. The U.S.-EU divergence has affected progress in a number of institutions, including the UN, the WTO, the NPT, and the International Criminal Court (ICC).

New rising powers such as China and India will also challenge the premises of AIM thinking. These countries have immense populations and are growing quickly in economic might. They retain some traits and preferences of developing countries, but are gaining the political weight of developed countries. They have good historical reasons to be dissatisfied with the current distribution of power in the American-built system and good reasons to join as well.

China, for example, has often not thrived under Western hegemony—that is, in its "century of humiliation." It has portrayed itself as the champion of the third world. Yet it has also been on the UN Security Council, has benefited from economic liberalization in the AIM world, and increasingly attends the G-8, the elite club of super-rich nations. Because of its crossover identity as developing country and superpower, and especially because of its snowballing economic clout, China will be increasingly important in the governance of world politics.

The issue for the United States and the fortunes of its AIM thinking is that the deals it will want to cut and what others are willing to agree to have shifted and are due to shift more. Americans believe that a return to AIM will help them get what they want through better diplomacy. But it will take more than diplomacy to conclude new major agreements. Other countries will likely demand more inclusion for their interests, and their values may differ from the current ones. What is not clear is whether Americans are willing to cut deals that allow for those differences or whether they can seal deals when interests overlap.

In the past, U.S. economic and military resources were often used to paper over gaps in values and interests and get deals done.[26] The United States had a surplus of economic and military goodies that gave it great leverage. Today it retains military might that still provides influence, but its relative economic clout has weakened. The United States faces significant constraints in the form of budget and international deficits, it has challengers in the global marketplace (such as the EU), the power of the dollar has waned, and the technological lead of the U.S. economy is smaller than it used to be. Yes, the United States still has leverage, but it is unclear whether it is enough.

Cutting deals to establish order will require more and greater concessions on the part of traditional U.S. interests (for example, deals with an authoritarian China). This could begin to hit home when even a skillful diplomacy by a popular leader encounters other significant countries that nonetheless are still unwilling to agree to the U.S. agenda. Hence over the longer term the friction caused by the shortfall between expectations and results will be a potential source of change and an opening for reengineering U.S. foreign policy.

Alternatives to AIM

Of course, whether major changes are realized depends as much on there being a new foreign policy as it does on the implosion of the old policy. It is not possible to change from something to nothing. In the absence of some approach that has political support and that offers a solution to the problems faced, countries have sometimes stuck with the old ideas regardless of their fit with the circumstances.[27]

One of the reasons the Bush revolution was even possible as an experiment was because a dedicated and energetic set of social activists—commonly referred to as neoconservatives—had developed and promulgated a coherent worldview in the 1990s.[28] These thinkers held influence and positions in the government in the Bush administration. Thus when the 9/11 attacks unsettled the commitment to the AIM ideas, they had an approach ready to go that could replace it.

Today it is not clear what strategy will take the place of AIM. The two alternatives from America's past—a type of neo-isolationism or a new manifestation of American nationalism akin to the Bush doctrine—have their advocates, but both appear to be minority positions. Intellectuals are again arguing over, and attempting to build support for, new alternative strategies.[29] Yet because there is little consensus around any particular vision, the absence of a viable alternative strategy may be the most difficult hurdle in the way of a transformation of U.S. policy.

Implications for Policy Planning

If this portrait of U.S. foreign policy has any validity, then the main tasks for policy planning in the years ahead will lie in three areas: implementing the AIM policy; attending to the fallout from the shortfall of expectations; and helping to nurture longer-term alternatives.

First, AIM is not dead, and it is the best feasible framework that exists today. Still, policy planners will have to help resolve the important debates about the most effective way to implement the consensus behind leadership, military preponderance, democratization, economic integration, and cooperation. As noted there are significant and serious divides about how to do this, and policy planning can help governments pressed by immediate challenges understand which choices have better long-term prospects.

Policy planning might also play a role in managing the failed expectations that are likely to result from that implementation. In the past, presidents have often exaggerated challenges and overpromised, with deleterious effects on strategy. Woodrow Wilson overpromised on the results from intervening in World War I. Yet people's expectations went unfulfilled and disillusionment set in, internationalism suffered, and throughout the interwar years the United

States was constrained from playing a constructive role in the international system. After the 9/11 attacks, President Bush also sought to steel Americans' attention around a terrorist threat of global reach. That focus mobilized a consensus behind military intervention in Afghanistan and then in Iraq, but the rhetoric also may have blurred critical distinctions (between terrorist and insurgent) in a way that stymied those conflicts and the broader campaign against Al Qaeda.

Finally, policy planning can play a role in generating new paradigms in U.S. foreign policy thinking both inside and outside the government. The goal would be to help nurture a base for policies that might one day replace the current orthodoxy. Admittedly this is a more difficult and nondoctrinaire use of policy planning, but there are some precedents. For example, Franklin Roosevelt and his administration, in conjunction with societal actors, did much to nurture support for American internationalism, even as popular sentiment and most of the policies of his early years as president favored the then dominant "no-entanglement" approach to U.S. foreign policy.[30]

In the 1920 election, Warren Harding promised a "return to normalcy" after all the turbulence of Wilson's presidency. In the 2008 election, both John McCain and Barack Obama pledged a return to the "normalcy" of American internationalism following the rollercoaster of the Bush doctrine. Yet just as Harding's embrace of tradition ("no entanglement") was not suited to the international conditions the United States faced in the interwar period, so too is the U.S. embrace of AIM likely to be increasingly at odds with the emerging conditions the country will confront in the years ahead. At a minimum U.S. leaders will need to reorient public expectations for AIM and recognize the necessity to cut deals, in light of pressing problems, that may involve more give from the United States than has been necessary since World War II.

The challenges for policy planning are those that confront the country beyond the short term. An increasingly complex and dynamic world makes designing foreign policy a difficult task. But that same complexity also makes the need for understanding and charting possible futures more important. Government officials with pressing daily demands can rarely look too far ahead; still, as George Kennan illustrated in his logic of containment, a long-term view can be essential to successful strategy.

Notes

1. On polarization see Charles Kupchan and Peter Trubowitz, "Dead Center: The Demise of Liberal Internationalism in the United States," *International Security* 32, no. 2 (2007): 7–44.

2. In the Americas, the United States has been more prone to using overt force for democratization efforts. In other places it has tended to rely on political, economic, and covert means.

3. See, for example, Thomas Kean and Lee Hamilton, *The 9/11 Commission Final Report* (Washington: Government Printing Office, 2004), pp. 399ff (www.gpoaccess.gov/911/Index.html [December 22, 2008]).

4. For a fuller exposition of this issue, see Jeffrey W. Legro, *Rethinking the World: Great Power Strategies and International Order* (Cornell University Press, 2005).

5. See Kean and Hamilton, *The 9/11 Commission Final Report*, esp. chap. 11, "Foresight—and Hindsight."

6. John Lewis Gaddis, "A Grand Strategy of Transformation," *Foreign Policy* (November–December 2002): 50.

7. Melvyn P. Leffler, "9/11 and the Past and Future of the U.S. Foreign Policy," *International Affairs* 79, no. 5 (October 2003): 1045–63; John Lewis Gaddis, *Surprise, Security, and the American Experience* (Yale University Press, 2004).

8. See Philip Zelikow, "The Transformation of National Security," *National Interest*, no. 71 (Spring 2003): 17–30; he noted, "The Bush administration has helped spur a worldwide debate not only about the purposes of American power, but about the objectives of the international system as a whole."

9. John McCain, "An Enduring Peace Built on Freedom," *Foreign Affairs* (November/December 2007): 19–34; Barack Obama, "Renewing America's Leadership," *Foreign Affairs* (July/August 2007): 2–16.

10. See, for example, Mike Allen and Romesh Ratnesar, "The End of Cowboy Diplomacy," *Time*, July 9, 2006; and Philip H. Gordon, "The End of the Bush Revolution," *Foreign Affairs* (July/August 2006): 75–86.

11. Melvyn P. Leffler and Jeffrey W. Legro, eds., *To Lead the World: U.S. Strategy after the Bush Doctrine* (Oxford University Press, 2008).

12. Chicago Council on Global Affairs, Public Opinion Study, 2006 (www.world publicopinion.org/pipa/articles/brunitedstatescanadara/256.php?nid=&id=&pnt=256 &lb=brusc [December 9, 2008]).

13. Ibid.

14. Chicago Council on Global Affairs, "Globalization and Trade," April 2007 (www.worldpublicopinion.org/pipa/articles/btglobalizationtradera/349.php?nid=&id =&pnt=349&lb=btgl [December 9, 2008]).

15. "Comprehensive Analysis of Polls Reveals Americans' Attitudes on U.S. Role in the World," WorldPublicOpinion.org, August 3, 2007 (www.worldpublicopinion.org/ pipa/articles/brunitedstatescanadara/383.php?lb=brusc&pnt=383&nid=&id=) and "United Nations" (www.americans-world.org/digest/global_issues/un/un1.cfm [December 9, 2008]).

16. See Melvyn P. Leffler and Jeffrey W. Legro, "Dilemmas of Strategy," in *To Lead the World*, edited by Leffler and Legro, pp. 250–76.

17. See, for example, John Lewis Gaddis, *Strategies of Containment* (Oxford University Press, 1982).

18. Michael G. Krukones, *Promises and Performance: Presidential Campaigns as Policy Predictors* (Lanham, Md.: University Press of America, 1984), esp. pp. 123–25.

19. Jeff Fishel, *Presidents and Promises: From Campaign Pledges to Presidential Performance* (Washington: Congressional Quarterly Press, 1985); Ian Budge and Richard I. Hofferbert, "Mandates and Policy Outputs: U.S. Party Platforms and Federal Expenditures," *American Political Science Review* 84, no. 1 (March 1990): 111–31.

20. For more on these debates see Leffler and Legro, "Dilemmas of Strategy."

21. Kishore Mahbubani, "The Impending Demise of the Postwar System," *Survival* 47, no. 4 (2005): 7–18; G. John Ikenberry, "A Weaker World," *Prospect* (November 2005): 30–33; James G. Poulos, "The Exhaustion of the International Order," *American Spectator Online,* March 14, 2006; Hanns Maull, "The Precarious State of International Order," *Asia-Pacific Review* (2006): 68–77.

22. See, for example, the writings of John Ikenberry.

23. See Hedley Bull, *The Anarchical Society* (Columbia University Press, 1977); Daniel Drezner, *All Politics Is Global: Explaining International Regulatory Regimes* (Princeton University Press, 2007).

24. Robert Kagan, "Power and Weakness: Why the United States and Europe See the World Differently," *Policy Review,* no. 113 (June and July 2002): 3–28.

25. John Peterson and Michael E. Smith, "The EU as a Global Actor," in *The European Union: How Does It Work?* edited by Elizabeth Bomberg and Alexander Stubb, pp. 195–215 (Oxford University Press, 2002).

26. See, for example, Robert Gilpin, *The Political Economy of International Relations* (Princeton University Press, 1987); Michael Mandelbaum, *The Case for Goliath: How America Acts as the World's Government in the Twenty-First Century* (New York: Public Affairs, 2005).

27. This was the case with Tokugawa Japan in the 1800s, and then with China later in the century. The U.S. aversion to entanglement in great-power politics, even when it was the greatest power after World War I, also has some of these tendencies.

28. See, for example, Stefan Halper and Jonathan Clarke, *America Alone: The Neo-Conservatives and the Global Order* (Cambridge University Press, 2005).

29. For example, Fareed Zakaria, *The Post-American World* (New York: W. W. Norton, 2008); Robert Kagan, *The Return of History and the End of Dreams* (New York: Knopf, 2008). Also see the Center for a New American Security's "Solarium II" project (www.cnas.org/solarium2/ [December 9, 2008]).

30. Robert A. Divine, *Second Chance: The Triumph of Internationalism in America during World War II* (New York: Athenaeum, 1967); Inderjeet Parmar, "Engineering Consent: The Carnegie Endowment for International Peace and the Mobilization of American Public Opinion, 1939–1945," *Review of International Studies* (2000): 35–48.

PART
III

Reforming
Strategic Planning

BRUCE W. JENTLESON

5

An Integrative Executive Branch Strategy for Policy Planning

Getting policy planning right within the State Department is hard enough. But it's not enough. There also needs to be a better executive branch–wide process, systematically integrating policy planning across State, Defense, the intelligence community, Treasury, and other key departments and agencies and structurally linking them to the National Security Council (NSC).

The challenges—analytic, organizational, political—of devising an integrative executive branch policy planning strategy that is not just neatly rational on paper but effective in practice are not to be underestimated. Nor, though, is the need. Good policy planning is not a sufficient condition for successful foreign policy. But it is a necessary one, especially for a new administration facing as full and complex an agenda as the Obama administration does, and doing so in such highly transitional times.

Both points are stressed by academics and practitioners, Democrats and Republicans. Andrew Bennett and I earlier wrote that policy planning is treated too much as an oxymoron and too little as a sine qua non.[1] Aaron Friedberg puts it most starkly: "The U.S. government has lost the capacity to conduct serious, sustained national strategic planning. . . . At a minimum, the absence of an institutionalized planning process seems certain to lead to a loss of efficiency: misallocated resources, suboptimal policies, duplication of effort, lost opportunities, and costly improvisations. At worst, it raises the risk of catastrophic failure."[2]

The first section of this chapter sets the context through analysis of the principal recurring dilemmas for policy planning, drawing mostly on the experience of the State Department policy planning staff (S/P) but also on the

Defense Department, the intelligence community, and other executive branch actors. The second section presents the integrative executive branch policy planning strategy in both its structure and its process. The third section lays out an initial substantive agenda for policy planning in a new administration.

Recurring Dilemmas in Policy Planning

Foreign policy planning has four main components and considerations: planning for policy; planning and operational roles; planning within a bureaucracy; and political constraints.

Planning for Policy

Back in April 1947 when they created the State Department policy planning staff (S/P), Secretary of State George Marshall and founding policy planning director George Kennan had a keen sense of the need for broad strategic thinking in times of global transition. Secretary Marshall laid out the original mandate in a memo: (1) formulate and develop long-term policies; (2) anticipate potential threats and challenges; (3) conduct studies on broad political-military issues; (4) assess current policy and make advisory recommendations as to its adequacy; (5) coordinate planning within State. There also was his powerfully succinct charge, "avoid trivia," in effect in caps and boldface.[3]

Although the mandate was to look at a bigger picture than had been standard practice, the task was not about formulating a grandiose overarching doctrine for American foreign policy. All those who look at that period with "containment envy" need to bear this in mind. As history it is way too rose-colored, forgetting the nonuniversality of containment that Kennan himself so often stressed and the major policy failures in Vietnam and elsewhere that resulted when Kennan's advice was ignored. As precedent it encourages efforts to articulate successor policies that either don't stick (such as enlargement in the early Clinton administration) or do more harm than good (such as the Bush administration's era-defining version of the war on terrorism).

The same goes for eschewing academic formulations of "grand strategy" or "general theory," ironclad laws or grandiose dictums. Rather than a genuinely guiding and overarching framework at the time, past grand strategy has been made grander by what gets read into it retrospectively. As to general theory, Alexander George once remarked that there's no surer way to get eyes to glaze over in the policy world than to use the "t word."[4] Even in the academic world the "-isms debates" are starting to be seen more for their parochialism than for their erudition.

Still, foreign policy strategy cannot be just a list of issues and positions formulated on an ad hoc basis in response to events. It needs a conceptual dimension. Part of the value of providing such a perspective is diagnostic, to help policymakers assess the nature of the problems they face, the trends they are observing, the warning signs they may be sensing. Often the problem is less a dearth than a glut of information, and the need is to discern patterns, establish salience, and trace causal connections. It is one thing, for example, to come up with an exhaustive list of factors and conditions that are associated with the causes of war. It is quite another to home in on key factors that are sufficiently broad to provide a sound analytic basis for policy planning but sufficiently finite to be manipulated and influenced by policy instruments. Similarly, learning from history can be diagnostically helpful as long as the lessons drawn are analytically sound and reasonably specified.[5]

Such thinking also can have prescriptive value to the extent that it includes "the conceptualization of strategies." Such analysis, while not directly operational, "identifies the critical variables of a strategy and the general logic associated with [its] successful use."[6] For example:

—Under what conditions are economic sanctions most likely to be effective?

—What are the key factors that usually affect the success of democracy promotion strategies?

—What lessons can be drawn from other regions for building regional security institutions in the Middle East?

This kind of formulation may not tell us with certainty whether a particular foreign policy strategy is going to succeed. But when combined with analysis specific to the issue at hand, it can tell us which factors and what conditions are most conducive to policy success.

That said, there's no substitute for timing. Based on his experience, Stephen Krasner sees the process as much more opportunistic than orderly.[7] He recounts how his being in the right place at the right time—in one instance, sitting in a van with the assistant secretary of state for public affairs outside the venue where Secretary of State Condoleezza Rice was giving a speech—was key in getting "traction" for ideas that became crucial for the Partnership for Democratic Governance.[8] In another instance it was a memo on relations with China beyond the standard containment-engagement framework that had sat in the desk of an S/P staffer for three years until Robert Zoellick became deputy secretary of state; the analysis resonated with Zoellick and became the basis for the "responsible stakeholder" formulation that went on to show substantial staying power. In both of these instances, though, had not the conceptual and analytic work already been done and done well, the window of opportunity would have been there, but no ideas ready enough to push through.

In this regard it is useful to keep in mind President Dwight Eisenhower's oft-quoted distinction between policy plans themselves, which can never adequately foresee all possible contingencies, and strategic thinking, which is useful even if specific plans must be adapted. "The plans are nothing," he put it, "but the planning is everything."[9]

Planning and Operational Roles

Part of the tension in foreign policy planning is between today and tomorrow. Marshall very much had tomorrow in mind, looking "not into the distant future, but beyond the vision of the operating officers caught in the smoke and crises of current battle; far enough ahead to see the emerging form of things to come and outline what should be done to meet or anticipate them."[10] This kind of strategic analysis requires sufficient distancing from the day-to-day operational aspects of policy to provide perspective and allow time for thought. On the other hand, unless planning has at least some direct bearing on the operational aspects of policy, S/P runs the risk of limited relevance. This in part is related to the generic organizational dilemma that, as James March and Herbert Simon put it, "daily routine drives out planning."[11] It is especially true in government, which as Richard Haass notes in his chapter is "an operational enterprise."

The literature on State S/P is replete with discussion of this problem. "Distraction lurks on two sides," Dean Acheson famously warned policy planners about veering too far toward operations on the one hand and "encyclopedism" on the other.[12] Robert Bowie, policy planning director in the Eisenhower administration and under Secretary of State John Foster Dulles, acknowledged that S/P "will have no special contribution to make if it becomes immersed in current activities," but also stressed that "if insights and thinking on long-term factors are to be effective, they must be brought to bear on such decisions as they are made."[13] Stephen Bosworth, planning director under President Reagan and Secretary of State George Shultz, makes the same point but with the emphases reversed, that while S/P "should not become yet one more aspirant for operational control over policy implementation, vying with the bureaus, neither should it become simply a long-range planning unit, producing intellectually interesting but basically irrelevant studies."[14] Lincoln Bloomfield stresses that "to be in the know, planners have to remain close to operations," while Robert Rothstein warns that "the planning staff buys influence at the cost of relinquishing the other roles it can play."[15]

The success that Kennan's S/P did have was due in significant part to balancing these planning and operational roles.[16] On the Marshall Plan, S/P worked to bring into the policy development process "the knowledge and views of all these people [State Department bureau officials], to cull out of them a workable recommendation for the principles on which our approach to this problem might be based and for the procedure that might best be followed."[17] Yet the reason the Kennan S/P example is so often cited is how rare other comparably successful instances have been.

In some respects the Department of Defense (DoD) does a better job of managing the planning-operational tension. War plans are developed well in advance through long processes that involve gaming, forecasting, force structure, contingency planning, and matching capabilities to doctrine. Broader defense doctrine and strategy, though, have encountered similar problems as at State—for example, as Andrew Bennett recounts, when DoD policy planning offices are diverted to immediate legislative and budgetary affairs, and subject to ebbs and flows of short-term appointments and leadership.[18]

Planning within a Bureaucracy

There are intradepartmental and interdepartmental aspects to planning within a bureaucracy. The intradepartmental one involves the fragmentation of policy planning among offices within the department. S/P is not the only planning unit within State. Regional and functional bureaus also have their own planning capacities. It would be neither feasible bureaucratically nor wise for policy to seek to eliminate such capacities. What S/P can do is position itself as the lead policy planning franchise but not the only one: "coordinate planning within State," as the Marshall-Kennan founding memo stated. S/P can best do this if its director is perceived as being very close to the secretary.[19] This creates incentives for worries about turf to be trumped by opportunities for access.

In DoD the internal fragmentation is even greater. In the current organizational structure policy planning has been split largely among three groups: (1) the principal assistant secretary of defense for policy planning, reporting to the principal deputy under secretary of defense for policy, reporting to the under secretary of defense for policy; (2) the deputy under secretary for planning, reporting to the under secretary of defense for personnel and readiness; and (3) the J-5 Strategic Plans and Policy Directorate, reporting to the director of the Joint Staff, reporting to the chairman of the Joint Chiefs of Staff.

The interdepartmental aspect is the typically limited planning coordination across departments and agencies. In addition to State and DoD, the National Intelligence Council has its own planning role. The Treasury Department has an Office of Policy Planning, although the director position has been combined with that of assistant secretary for public affairs—a flaw that is glaring in light of the 2008 financial crisis. The Commerce Department has an Office of Policy and Strategic Planning within the Office of the Secretary, structurally at least in this respect similar to State S/P. These may have been less important in earlier eras, but are more so today.

The best example of interdepartmental coordination was executed by the NSC Planning Board in the Eisenhower administration. Members were the lead planning officials from State, Defense, the Joint Chiefs of Staff, Treasury, and the CIA, with other departments and agencies involved according to the agenda. They met frequently, as often as two or three times per week. The mandate, according to Robert Bowie (who served on the Eisenhower NSC Planning Board) and historian Richard Immerman, was "establishing the general framework and goals of policy . . . [to] analyze trends, anticipate as well as identify problems, consider proposed solutions' advantages and disadvantages, and confront—explicitly—questions of means and ends." They also were charged with some planning-operational melding, taking "a new look at existing policies and programs." A balance was struck between emphasizing bureaucratic position, urging that Planning Board members be close to their respective principals, and averting bureaucratic parochialism, insisting that Planning Board members "seek with their background and experience statesman-like solutions to the problems of national security, rather than to reach solutions which represent merely a compromise of departmental positions."[20]

The Kennedy administration shifted the role of the NSC to make it more operational, which successor administrations largely continued. In his chapter in this book, Friedberg quotes Zbigniew Brzezinski as saying that "the Planning Board was a very important instrument, the elimination of which has handicapped the U.S. government ever since." In the Clinton administration some interagency policy planning was done on a project-specific basis, but not systematically, and was regularized as its own institutionalized interagency process. The Bush NSC created two NSC offices in the second term, Strategic Planning and Institutional Reform (SPIR) and Policy Implementation and Execution (PIE), which as Peter Feaver and Will Inboden recount in their chapter had some success, but only some. Based on his service on Vice

President Cheney's staff as well as his own scholarly perspective, Friedberg holds to the view that "to the extent that there has been something resembling a national strategic planning process in recent years, it has been run out of the vest pocket of the national security adviser. . . . Although NSC staff members have at times had titles that included the words 'strategic planning,' they have typically operated without significant staff support and have often been charged with other, more pressing duties, such as managing current policy issues or drafting speeches and other public documents that tend to take precedence over planning."

Political Constraints

Policy planning faces three principal political constraints that while not unique bear particularly on it. One is that politics is not only an operational business but a short-term one. Marshall's conception of looking even into the relatively near future often runs into political calendars. Not only are these short time frames, but in the American system they are staggered ones. Presidential electoral cycles feed thinking in four-year chunks, while Senate electoral cycles are six years and House of Representatives two. The national election schedule in parliamentary systems varies more, but at least everyone is elected at one time.

The second constraint is the risk that scenarios projected, critiques made, and options delineated as part of what is required for quality policy analysis may leak and cause political problems. This risk is even greater amidst the instantaneous and globalized dissemination that technology makes possible and the hyper-partisanship that often exists between political parties and among factions within political parties.[21] The qualifiers about analyzing, not advocating, tend to get drowned out by political bellicosity.

And third, even if public leaks are plugged, to the extent that planners try to alert policymakers to potential problems or crises, they risk career-damaging effects by being perceived as bearers of bad news or for crying wolf if the dangers warned of don't materialize. Although loyalty often is best demonstrated by constructive dissent, dissent often gets equated with disloyalty. Similarly, there is an imbalance between the incentives and disincentives of forewarning: it is difficult to know when deterrence or prevention has succeeded, and thus the rewards for being prescient are usually less than the penalties for crying wolf.

How can a new administration do better?

An Integrative Executive Branch Strategy: Structure and Process

The strategy that has the best chance of coping with the dilemmas inherent in foreign policy planning is an integrative executive branch–wide one that regularizes the coordination of policy planning across State, Defense, the intelligence community, Treasury, and other key departments and agencies and that is structurally linked to the National Security Council. Enhancing the role of State S/P is extremely important in its own right, and it should be part of this process. But the broad agenda (with fewer and fewer issues fitting neatly into diplomacy, defense, international economy, or other single categories), the array of other bureaucratic foreign–national security policy planning units, and the NSC's role as the hub (no matter what any administration may initially pledge about Cabinet government) make an institutionally integrated process essential.

The strategy I propose here involves creating a Strategic Planning Inter-Agency Group (SPIAG). Its membership would parallel the NSC structure: S/P director from State; principal deputy assistant secretary of defense for policy planning (from the Office of the Under Secretary of Defense for Policy); J-5 director from the Joint Chiefs of Staff; director of the National Intelligence Council; representation from Treasury by a new higher-ranking person whose planning duties are separate from public affairs; and a senior aide from the Office of the Vice President. Offices from other departments and agencies (Commerce, U.S. Trade Representative, Agency for International Development, Environmental Protection Agency, and Justice Department) would participate as warranted by the issue, as they currently do. A new NSC position, deputy national security adviser for strategic planning (DNSA-SP), would be created at a more senior level than any comparable position since the Eisenhower NSC Planning Board, with specific responsibilities distinct from those of the principal deputy national security adviser, including chairing the SPIAG.

This group would build on the Bush PIE and SPIR both with respect to what it succeeded in putting in place and in taking heed of the lessons Feaver and Inboden highlight. Of course it could be yet another overly organizationally rational structural reform that makes little difference. Interagency processes are notoriously slow and plodding when there's an issue in the in-box, let alone with the lessened time pressure of forward planning. The bureaucratic politics of each entity's role and expected contributions also often make it hard to put together a whole that is greater than the sum of its parts. Would SPIAG amount to anything more than another organizational chart that looks good on paper but bears little on practice?

Incentives need to guard against these natural tendencies. No incentive is more powerful than when a president makes it clear that something is a priority to him. While it's not the stuff of a major speech or full-court communications press, giving the creation of the SPIAG and the appointment of a DNSA-SP more than the typical attention at the start of a new administration would send a useful message. With that kind of launch, SPIAG would have a chance to cope effectively with the four recurring policy planning components.

Planning for Policy

Today's policy need for planning is at least as great as in the Marshall-Kennan early cold war times of transition. If there's one common theme among foreign policy professionals and scholars, it's the transitional nature of our times.[22] We don't need a single simple doctrine, but we do need a working understanding of the strategic context going forward.

We're not even sure of the structure of the system in which we seek to exert leadership.[23] It's not unipolar; it may have been for that "moment," but not the enduring and encompassing new system neoconservatives envisioned.[24] Nor is it just a matter of transitioning to a twenty-first-century version of nineteenth-century multipolarity, bringing China and India and a few others into the geopolitical hierarchy. With so many of the 190-plus nations in the world finally emerging on the global stage more assertive of their own interests and identities, and nonstate actors playing more significant roles for better (such as the Gates Foundation and its role in global health issues) or for worse (Al Qaeda), there's more to this evolving system than "pole-counting," uni- or multi-. While there's no expectation of a definitive formulation, a working sense of the broad systemic context can have real utility for specific policy questions.

With this and other aspects of the strategic context in mind, the memo launching SPIAG could be the original Marshall-Kennan one cited earlier, with but a few edits. The original mandate of formulating and developing long-term policies, anticipating potential threats and challenges, and assessing current policy and making advisory recommendations all still pertain. The portion on conducting studies on broad political-military issues needs to be broadened, and the planning coordination role should not be located just within State. The integrative structure helps to take into account the full range of factors across traditional issue area boundaries—a policy version of the multidisciplinarity starting to penetrate traditional disciplinary lines in academia.

Planning and Operational Roles

SPIAG's mandate must strike a balance such that planning is neither detached from nor consumed by operations. At the Tufts conference that led to the publication of this volume, James Steinberg, policy planning director in the first Clinton administration and deputy national security adviser in the second (and now deputy secretary of state), called this "bringing the future into the present," addressing long-term challenges in ways that relate them to immediate issues at hand.

The regularized and institutionalized link to the NSC can help with this planning-operational balance. As with all of foreign policy, little of a nonroutine nature happens unless the NSC helps make it happen.[25] Yet the NSC's increased influence has not been accompanied by any consistent role in coordinating policy planning. The very creation of the position of deputy national security adviser for strategic planning would make a statement about the priority being given to planning by a new administration. The position also would allow for direct access to the national security adviser, close collaboration with the deputy national security adviser, who typically chairs the Deputies Committee for high-priority immediate issues, and for interagency linkage at this level as well. It also could strengthen direct links to the Office of Management and Budget and its National Security Division, which is crucial for matching strategic planning with resource allocation.[26]

Planning within a Bureaucracy

Integrative executive branch policy planning strategy does not mean full melding. There are many issues on which State, DoD, Homeland Security, the intelligence community, Treasury, and others always will need to run their own policy planning, which, even when not totally self-contained, is more intra- than interagency. The purpose of SPIAG would be less consolidation than coordination, to institutionalize and make less ad hoc an interagency planning process.

SPIAG's creation can also have two other beneficial bureaucratic effects. One is as an incentive to departments and agencies to strengthen their own policy planning units and be effectively represented in the interagency process. The Eisenhower NSC Planning Board dictum about "statesman-like solutions" (rather than bureaucratic politics) still could be sustained, the point being to represent the viewpoint as effectively as possible in the integrative process. For Treasury this would be an incentive to separate policy planning from public affairs, and possibly elevate its stature by placing it closer to the Office of the Secretary. For DoD it could facilitate less internal fragmentation or at least a conferring of lead status on the office reporting to the under secretary for policy. At State it would make all the more important that the policy planning director have the confidence of and a close relationship with the secretary.

The other intradepartmental incentive would be to make the policy planning staff (not just the head position) more attractive to career officials within each department and agency once it has the higher priority and stature of an institutionalized and NSC-linked process. The bias toward operational responsibilities in promotion systems would still be there, but the gap would be lessened. Regular meetings at the White House and a new president whose initial interest in policy planning doesn't wane would similarly enhance incentives, including the sense of being "in the game," and could help attract high-quality noncareer appointees.

Political Constraints

The NSC link also could make for better coordination with political strategy both in terms of getting the buy-in needed for going from planning to policy and in inputting the political advice needed to build congressional and public support.

There is at least an argument that the political constraints caused by short-term considerations are loosening a bit. Some problems are beginning to be seen as the accumulated consequences of too much short-term thinking—for example, energy insecurity, climate change and environmental degradation, the financial bubble, and declining international economic competitiveness more broadly. Policy planners and political leaders can stop well short of being futurists or think tankers while still homing in on bringing the future into the present. Politics will never be a long-term business, but it can be more of a medium-term one.

Leaks and bearers of bad news will always exist, but processes can be structured to reduce them. Well-managed backup from political leaders can help.

Policy Planning Agenda for the New Administration

The new administration will need to start work early on its first National Security Strategy. A national security strategy must be issued; it is legislatively mandated. Often this gets treated as a let's-get-through-it exercise with more concern about saying too much than too little. Times of transition, though, make this more an opportunity than a burden.

A SPIAG blessed by the new president would be well positioned to run the national security strategy process. It would then be judged by how well it takes advantage of the opportunity. If the product is run-of-the-mill—unintegrated, nonstrategic, more an annotated list than a cohesive strategy—it will be relegated to the side role strategic planning typically has had. So too if it were to be too abstract and too future-oriented. But if a SPIAG were to produce a document with policy applicability and also political utility, it could build on that.

SPIAG also should focus on a few strategic initiatives that fit its mandate and comparative advantage. Four come to mind:

INTERNATIONAL ECONOMIC CRISIS. Even before the current economic crisis, there were numerous signs—the 1997 Asian financial crisis, the stalled-out WTO Doha Round, controversies over the World Bank, the ineffectiveness of the G-7 among them—of the inadequacies of key international institutions and policies. The scope and depth of the current crisis, and its potentially far-reaching geopolitical and security effects as well as economic ones, leave little doubt about the need for systemic reform. A U.S. strategy has to be an integrative one, for which the SPIAG structure is highly conducive. It also must be a bold one, addressing not only the immediate need for internationally coordinated relief and stabilization but helping lay the groundwork for institutions and processes with the capacity to meet the challenges of globalization and its interconnectedness.

CLIMATE CHANGE AND ENERGY SECURITY. "Self-help" is among the oldest axioms of international relations. Although it usually refers to military power and national defense, it especially pertains to the vulnerability that we have self-inflicted by our oil addiction. With fluctuating gasoline prices and natural disasters hitting the United States with a severity and frequency that defies historical patterns, climate change and energy security finally have an immediacy and a national interest relevance in the minds of the American public to go with the longer-term and more broadly global concerns. For a new U.S. administration to go from laggard to leader on global climate change would be a powerful statement. The same sheer size that has made the United States such a major part of the problem can make it a major part of the solution. The complexity of doing so—economically, technologically, and politically; in the public sector, private sector, and nonprofit sector; nationally and internationally—makes this perhaps the ultimate strategic challenge. SPIAG's role would hardly suffice. But it would be necessary for breaking out of what has been a much too incremental approach that has not provided the reach to match the scope of the problem.

MIDDLE EAST REGIONAL SECURITY. The Middle East tends to be approached by issue: Israeli-Palestinian peace and security, Iraq, Iran, Lebanon. But while each of these has plenty of issue-specific elements, all also affect and are affected by broader issues of regional security. The Bush I administration understood the regional dimensions back in 1991 when it initiated Middle East multilateral working groups as part of the Madrid peace process on arms control and regional security and other areas.[27] While others in the U.S. government take the lead on more focused and immediate aspects of these issues, SPIAG would focus on regional security strategies for both immediate tie-ins (for example, regional security proposals being made to Iran as part of the nonproliferation negotiations) and longer-term development of a regional security regime.

GENOCIDE PREVENTION AND OTHER HUMANITARIAN INTERVENTION. As with many such election-year task forces, the bipartisan Genocide Prevention Task Force sought to elevate an issue in importance and provide policy recommendations as well as some political basis for a new administration to act.[28] Darfur is the immediate issue at hand and will require less strategic planning than operational planning. SPIAG's main role would be to help develop a strategy with which the United States could play a leadership role in moving "the responsibility to protect" from rhetoric to reality.[29] This is needed not just for humanitarian reasons but also to further other policy objectives given the ramifications such conflicts have had for regional stability, terrorism safe havens, and other concerns.

Policy Planning in the "Real World"

The academic community often gets derided by the policy community as not living in the "real world." Many such criticisms are warranted. But I find myself also sometimes asking just how real a world is that sticks to policies and policy processes, knowing that they don't work very well and that there is a real need for ones that work better. Academics may overestimate the ease of change; but politicians often underestimate the consequences of more of the same.

The integrative executive branch policy planning strategy proposed herein may not get it exactly right. Better ideas are welcome. But the debate needs to shift from *if* more effective policy planning is possible to *how* to make it possible. The agenda is full. The issues are complex. The pace is intense. The competition is tough. Effective strategic planning will not guarantee foreign policy success—but foreign policy success is much less likely without it.

Notes

1. See Bruce W. Jentleson and Andrew Bennett, "Policy Planning: Oxymoron or Sine Qua Non for U.S. Foreign Policy?" in *Good Judgment in Foreign Policy: Theory and Application,* edited by Stanley A. Renshon and Deborah Welch Larson, pp. 219–45 (Boulder, Colo.: Westview Press, 2003), on which this chapter draws.

2. See Aaron L. Friedberg, "Strengthening U.S. Strategic Planning," *Washington Quarterly* 31, no. 1 (Winter 2007–08): 47, as well as his chapter in this book. See also Michèle A. Flournoy and Shawn W. Brimley, "Strategic Planning for National Security: A New Project Solarium," *Joint Forces Quarterly,* no. 41 (Spring 2006): 80–86.

3. George F. Kennan, *Memoirs, 1925–1950* (Boston: Little, Brown, 1967), pp. 326–27.

4. Alexander L. George, *Bridging the Gap: Theory and Practice in Foreign Policy* (Washington: U.S. Institute of Peace Press, 1993).

5. Richard Neustadt and Ernest May, *Thinking in Time: The Uses of History for Decisionmaking* (New York: Free Press, 1986); Yuen Foong Khong, *Analogies at War: Korea, Munich, Dien Bien Phu, and the Vietnam Decision of 1965* (Princeton University Press, 1992).

6. George, *Bridging the Gap,* pp. 117–18.

7. See Krasner's chapter in this volume.

8. This timing was enhanced by this being an issue on which he brought to his position as S/P director ideas from his scholarly work; see, for example, Stephen Krasner, "Sharing Sovereignty: New Institutions for Collapsed and Failing States," *International Security* 29, no. 2 (Fall 2004): 85–120.

9. Robert R. Bowie and Richard H. Immerman, *Waging Peace: How Eisenhower Shaped an Enduring Cold War Strategy* (Oxford University Press, 1998), p. vii.

10. Dean Acheson, *Present at the Creation: My Years in the State Department* (New York: W. W. Norton, 1969), p. 214.

11. Cited in Robert L. Rothstein, *Planning, Prediction and Policy-Making in Foreign Affairs* (Boston: Little, Brown, 1972), p. 84.

12. Acheson, *Present at the Creation,* p. 214.

13. Cited in Rothstein, *Planning, Prediction and Policy-Making,* p. 62, n. 71.

14. Cited in Lucian Pugliaresi and Diane T. Berliner, "Policy Analysis at the Department of State: The Policy Planning Staff," *Journal of Policy Analysis and Management* 8, no. 3 (1989): 381.

15. Lincoln Bloomfield, "Planning Foreign Policy: Can It Be Done?" *Political Science Quarterly* 93, no. 3 (Fall 1978): 376–77; Rothstein, *Planning, Prediction and Policy-Making,* p. 61.

16. When Kennan stepped down as S/P director in 1949, he did so with some despondence, writing in his diary that he and his staff had "simply been a failure, like all previous attempts to bring order and foresight into the designing of foreign policy

by special institutional arrangement within the department." While some of this can be written off as Kennan's characteristic crustiness, it is also a useful corrective to over-glorifying those early cold war days. Kennan, *Memoirs,* p. 467. Anthony Lake, S/P director in the Carter administration (1977–81), recounts having lunch with Kennan, seeking his advice, and Kennan's saying, "Worst job I ever had" (personal communication, April 2008).

17. Kennan, *Memoirs,* p. 343.

18. See Jentleson and Bennett, "Policy Planning," drawing on Bennett's experience as a member of the DoD Plans and Analysis Group under Assistant Secretary of Defense for International Security Affairs Joseph S. Nye Jr. in 1994–95.

19. In addition to the close Marshall-Kennan relationship, other closely cooperative secretary-S/P director relationships were those between Henry Kissinger and Winston Lord, Cyrus Vance and Anthony Lake, James Baker and Dennis Ross, Warren Christopher and James Steinberg, and Colin Powell and Richard Haass.

20. Bowie and Immerman, *Waging Peace,* pp. 91–92.

21. Ronald Brownstein, *The Second Civil War: How Extreme Partisanship Has Paralyzed Washington and Polarized America* (New York: Penguin Press, 2007).

22. See, for example, Fareed Zakaria, *The Post-American World* (New York: W. W. Norton, 2008), Kishore Mahbubani, *The New Asian Hemisphere: The Irresistible Shift of Global Power to the East* (New York: Public Affairs, 2008); Richard N. Haass, "The Age of Nonpolarity," *Foreign Affairs* 87, no. 3 (May/June 2008): 44–56; Bruce W. Jentleson and Steven Weber, "America's Hard Sell," *Foreign Policy* 169 (November/December 2008): 42–49.

23. Bruce W. Jentleson, "America's Global Role after Bush," *Survival* 49, no. 3 (Autumn 2007): 179–99.

24. Charles Krauthammer, "The Unipolar Moment," *Foreign Affairs* (Winter 1990/91): 23–33, and "The Unipolar Moment Revisited," *National Interest* 70 (Winter 2002/03): 5–17.

25. David J. Rothkopf, *Running the World: The Inside Story of the National Security Council and the Architects of American Power* (New York: Public Affairs, 2005); Ivo H. Daalder and I. M. Destler, *In the Shadow of the Oval Office: From JFK to Bush II—The National Security Advisor* (New York: Simon and Schuster, 2009).

26. See Gordon Adams, "Rebalancing and Integrating the National Security Toolkit," testimony to the Senate Foreign Relations Committee, April 24, 2008.

27. Dalia Dassa Kaye, *Beyond the Handshake: Multilateral Cooperation in the Arab-Israeli Peace Process, 1991–1996* (Columbia University Press, 2001).

28. Madeleine K. Albright and William S. Cohen, *Preventing Genocide: A Blueprint for U.S. Policymakers* (Washington: U.S. Holocaust Memorial Museum, American Academy of Diplomacy, and Endowment of the U.S. Institute of Peace, 2008).

29. Gareth Evans, *The Responsibility to Protect: Ending Mass Atrocities Once and for All* (Washington: Brookings, 2008).

AARON L. FRIEDBERG

6

Strengthening U.S. Strategic Planning

The U.S. government has lost the capacity to conduct serious, sustained national strategic planning. Although there are offices and bureaus scattered throughout the executive branch that perform parts of this task for their respective agencies, there is no one place where all the pieces are brought together and integrated into anything resembling a coherent, comprehensive whole. What is worse, to judge by the tentative and incomplete efforts that have been made thus far to correct this shortcoming, there appears to be very little concern about what it may mean for the nation's security.

These institutional and intellectual deficiencies have existed for some time and cannot be blamed on the Bush administration or its immediate predecessors. Nevertheless, the consequences of an eroding capacity for strategic planning, and an apparently dwindling recognition at the highest levels of government of its importance, have become painfully evident in recent years. At a minimum, the absence of an institutionalized planning process seems certain to lead to a loss of efficiency: misallocated resources, suboptimal policies, duplication of effort, lost opportunities, and costly improvisations. At worst, it raises the risk of catastrophic failure.

Although the problem is deeply rooted and no perfect solution exists, significant improvements are possible. These will require changes not only in organization but also in the mind-set of officials at all levels of the national security system. Even the most strategically inclined top officials cannot do serious planning on their own without a staff and a process to support them. On the other hand, adding planning bureaus is pointless if leaders refuse to use them or to take them seriously.

Planning, Not Plans

National strategic challenges must be met by the application of all the instruments of national power—including diplomacy, financial pressure and economic inducements, information operations, and covert action, as well as the threat or use of military force—and therefore require cooperation among executive branch departments and agencies.

Such challenges may vary in scope and duration, but their defining feature is the demand they impose for coordination in planning and execution. The ongoing efforts to stabilize Iraq and to block or dismantle the Iranian and North Korean nuclear programs are critically important national strategic challenges of comparatively limited geographic scope and likely duration. Each will play out, one way or another, over the next several years. By contrast, winning the "long war" against violent Islamist groups and preventing the further spread of weapons of mass destruction will require policies coordinated on a global scale and over a period of decades. The rise of China may be the greatest challenge confronting the United States in Asia and beyond in the coming century. In an ideal world, the U.S. approaches to these interrelated issues should be coordinated and synchronized. At a minimum, they should be designed and executed so as not to conflict with one another.

The purpose of a national strategic planning process is not to produce a single, comprehensive document, an assortment of paper plans for subsidiary challenges, or an endless array of specific contingencies. The proper aim of such a process is not really to generate plans at all, but rather to inform and support the deliberations of top executive branch officials as they make strategic decisions. The true aim of national strategic planning is heuristic; it is an aid to collective thinking at the highest echelons of the government, rather than a mechanism for the production of operational plans. This point is nicely captured in President Dwight Eisenhower's pithy observation that whereas "plans are useless . . . planning is indispensable."[1]

Four Key Tasks

When General George Marshall established the Department of State's policy planning staff in 1947, he had in mind that it would perform two distinct tasks. The first was "to look ahead, not into the distant future, but beyond the vision of the operating officers caught in the smoke and crises of current battle; far enough ahead to see the emerging form of things to come and outline what should be done to meet or anticipate them." At the same time, "the staff should also do something else—constantly reappraise what [is] being done."[2] Marshall's broad categories of assessment and anticipation can be further divided into four specific functions: weighing alternative strategies, assessing current strategy, examining high-impact contingencies, and identifying key trends and emerging issues.

The first and most fundamental task of any strategic planning operation is to develop alternative courses of action and to assist policymakers in conducting a systematic evaluation of their potential costs and benefits. Because the responses of the opponent and the unfolding of events can never be predicted with assurance, this kind of calculation is always imprecise and becomes even more so the farther into the future it attempts to project. Yet for nations as well as individuals, some attempt to identify and evaluate different paths forward is the sine qua non of rational behavior.

Ideally, a rigorous assessment of alternatives should be undertaken before a strategy is chosen or, in the event that an existing approach is deemed ineffective, before a change is initiated. Unfortunately, real-life decisionmaking usually bears little resemblance to theoretical models. If it happens at all, the process of examining alternative courses of action may be truncated, unsystematic, or biased by the fact that the "right" answer is already known. Although no bureaucratic mechanism can provide absolute protection against such failings, the absence of any process at all makes them far more likely.

Because strategic interaction involves a contest of adversaries' wills, it is rarely sufficient for one side or the other simply to choose a path and then to stick to it until it has reached its goal. Unless the opponent is completely outmatched or virtually inert, his reactions, countermoves, and initiatives will almost always call for adjustments and sometimes entirely new approaches. Without an ongoing effort to assess how a struggle is unfolding, it will be impossible to make the tactical shifts or wholesale changes in strategy necessary to increase the odds of success. Although it is always conceivable that a combatant may stumble into victory simply by "staying the course," there is also the danger of blundering into defeat. Like a sailor in heavy winds and high seas who fails to consult his sextant and compass, a nation that does not regularly assess the performance of its strategy and that of its opponent is likely to wander far from its intended destination.

As obvious as these points might seem, governments, having chosen a course of action, often do not engage in rigorous analysis of the sort that could help them to assess their performance and even at times avoid disaster. One important purpose of a strategic planning process is therefore to assist top decisionmakers in engaging in this kind of ongoing evaluation of existing policies, and if necessary to help them force the rest of government to do the same.

Lurking just beyond the "smoke and crises of current battle" is an array of developments that could change its course. These typically involve actions taken by an adversary (or sometimes by an ally or third party), but they may also be events that, despite being exogenous to it, could nevertheless reshape an ongoing strategic interaction. Planners cannot reasonably be expected to anticipate and analyze every conceivable contingency, but they should be able to select a finite number that, either because of their plausibility, their likely effects, or some combination of the two, would demand a significant response. Top decisionmakers are usually aware of at least some of these possibilities and may even have given preliminary consideration to a few of them. They are unlikely, however, to have had the time to work through the implications of specific contingencies in a structured way and still less likely to have made any initial judgments about how to proceed should a particular high-impact event occur. Another aim of a national-level strategic planning process should therefore be to assist decisionmakers in identifying key contingencies, assessing the dangers and opportunities they might present, selecting those that require further detailed planning and preparation, and making preliminary decisions about how to respond should one of them arise.

Even if planners cannot see far enough ahead to anticipate with great precision the "form of things to come," they can often identify key trends and emerging issues of potential significance for ongoing or possible future strategic interactions. The final aim of a national-level strategic planning mechanism should be to bring these developments to the attention of top decisionmakers and to assist them in thinking through their potential implications.

As with more narrowly defined, nearer-term contingencies, it is likely that top decisionmakers are aware of at least some important trends and potential emerging issues. Yet given their comparative lack of urgency and uncertainties about their eventual emergence and potential significance, it is far less probable that these will have received systematic consideration anywhere in the government, to say nothing of its uppermost reaches.

Obstacles to Implementation

At least three sets of barriers stand in the way of strengthening the U.S. government's capacity to conduct strategic planning: bureaucratic, political, and intellectual.

Notional Examples

- *Weighing alternative strategies.* Before confronting Pyongyang with evidence that it had a secret uranium enrichment project in autumn 2002: undertake an analysis of broad alternative approaches to compelling the North to abandon its nuclear weapons programs.
- *Assessing current strategy.* Following the initiation of Six-Party Talks in spring/summer 2003: perform periodic assessments of whether the process of multilateral negotiations was working, based on prior analysis of the assumptions on which the strategy was based and explicit identification of indicators of progress (or its absence).
- *Examining key contingencies.* At any point in the process: conduct an analysis of the likely impact of a North Korean nuclear weapons test and possible alternative U.S. responses to it.
- *Identifying emerging issues.* At any point in the process: begin to analyze the long-term implications for the United States of a more highly proliferated world.

Bureaucratic interests

Within the existing organizational structure of the federal government, the National Security Council (NSC) is the logical home for a national strategic planning mechanism. As has already been noted, the executive branch organizations engaged in the formulation and implementation of national security policy—primarily the State, Defense, Commerce, and Treasury Departments, the individual armed services, the Joint Staff, and the intelligence agencies—all have some capacity for strategic planning, but these units naturally focus on the concerns of their home departments. It is only within the Executive Office of the President (EOP) that the different strands can be brought together and the activities of the various agencies orchestrated in accordance with some wider vision or plan.

The EOP has had little institutional capacity for strategic planning since the early 1960s, when the incoming Kennedy administration abolished the Eisenhower-era NSC Planning Board. The composition and functioning of this organization made it, in essence, a mechanism for performing the four functions of strategic planning. The Planning Board played a critical role during the 1950s, especially during the formative first term of Eisenhower's presidency. It ceased to function in the early 1960s, and from that point on the NSC largely abandoned its formal role as the locus for national strategic planning.

Beginning with the Kennedy administration, the national security adviser (NSA) and the NSC staff became preoccupied with the responsibility of supporting the president, managing crises, and overseeing and coordinating the day-to-day operations of the rest of the government. In the process, the ability of the NSA "to drive an extended iterative process of long-term strategic planning has simply been erased from the panoply of duties the position performs on a daily basis."[3] These responsibilities have not been picked up by any other office or agency. As former NSA Zbigniew Brzezinski remarked:

> The Planning Board was a very important instrument, the elimination of which has handicapped the U.S. government ever since then. Because the consequence is that we don't have overall national security planning. . . . There is a Policy Planning Council in the State Department, which has had its ups and downs. . . . The Defense Department can't plan national strategies. It's a military organization. And the White House doesn't do it anymore. . . . The NSC staff coordinates, but it has very little time for planning.[4]

To the extent that there has been something resembling a national strategic planning process in recent years, it has been run out of the vest pocket of the national security adviser, in small, informal clusters of top officials or, on some narrower issues, in ad hoc interagency working groups. Although there have at times been NSC staff members whose titles included the words "strategic planning," they have typically operated without significant staff support and have often been charged with more pressing duties, such as managing current policy issues or drafting speeches and other public documents, which tend to take precedence over planning. As Brzezinski explains: "One can have this or that senior staffer on the NSC try to do planning, but it's not the same thing" as a larger and more formal mechanism.[5]

Brzezinski tried to compensate for the absence of a developed planning process by hiring the distinguished Harvard political scientist Samuel Huntington. Following the reelection of President Bush, National Security Adviser Stephen Hadley made a similar move, creating a two-man Strategic Planning and Institutional Reform (SPIR) cell. The activities and accomplishments of this unit are described elsewhere in this volume. Notwithstanding the obvious dedication and ability of those assigned to it, SPIR's small size and relative isolation from the rest of the bureaucracy clearly placed significant limits on what it could accomplish.

Despite their inadequacy, arrangements in which high-level, interagency strategic planning units are either weak or nonexistent have evidently suited the bureaucratic interests of the most powerful players. There has rarely been any clamor for the creation of a more highly developed planning mechanism. The reasons are not difficult to discern. Strong national security advisers generally seek to retain tight control over policymaking and a short, uncluttered line of communication to the president. Opening the process up to include more agencies and departments would complicate deliberation and decisionmaking and reduce the independent power and importance of the NSA. On the other hand, when one or more of the departments is strong and the NSA is relatively weak, the department chiefs usually prefer to keep tight control of the parts of national policy that are within their respective domains. The absence of an authoritative strategic planning process makes it easier for them to do so.

Political Pressures

Broader domestic political considerations have tended to bolster these bureaucratic incentives. There is always a measure of tension and mistrust between elected and politically appointed officials and those who are part of the permanent, professional bureaucracy. The former often regard the latter as unimaginative, second-rate time-servers at best, and as disgruntled and potentially disloyal supporters of the party out of power at worst. The bureaucrats return the favor by viewing their superiors as amateurs and political hacks, if not wild-eyed ideologues of one stripe or another.

Because they often have little use for the bureaucracy, top-level officials may see scant need to create a planning process in which its collective views would be prominently featured. This inclination is reinforced by the fear of leaks or potentially embarrassing revelations by former government employees. The fact that it is now simply assumed that some of these people will immediately publish memoirs detailing the deliberations of which they were a part cannot help but have a chilling effect on discussions of strategy. The certain knowledge that those who quit and publish first will be the ones who are least happy with the direction of policy only strengthens the impulse to restrict serious deliberations to the innermost circle of political appointees.

The pervasive culture of leaks is another factor discouraging open, candid debate over the performance of existing strategies, the costs and benefits of possible alternatives, and potential responses to key contingencies or to emerging, longer-term trends. Those who disapprove of an existing strategy may try to discredit it by publicizing harsh internal assessments of its efficacy to date. Alternative strategies can sometimes be discredited before they have even been subjected to rigorous internal scrutiny if their outlines are revealed (often in distorted form) in the media. Two examples of this phenomenon are the leaks at the beginning of the Carter administration regarding possible force drawdowns in Europe, and those at the end of the George H. W. Bush administration regarding the possible desirability of a strategy aimed at preserving U.S. superiority by dissuading other countries from becoming military competitors. The mere fact that an administration is discussing certain courses of action, especially those that could involve the use of force, or even the possible strategic implications of long-term trends such as global warming, can be a cause of serious domestic and international embarrassment. For example, the revelation in 2004 that the Defense Department had sponsored research on the possible strategic implications of climate change caused a huge flap and no doubt discouraged future work on this important subject.

Although there is always some danger of exaggerating the extent to which standards of loyalty and discretion were higher in the past than they are today, there does appear to have been a marked decline in recent decades. In 1953 the Eisenhower administration's Project Solarium review of alternative grand strategies involved hundreds of people working over a period of months. Yet word of the existence of this review, to say nothing of its content, does not appear to have leaked. It is very hard to imagine that an equivalent effort could be carried out today with anything approaching this level of secrecy.

The strategic planning vacuum at the top of the executive branch organization chart could presumably be filled if the president and his chief advisers wanted it to be. Political considerations help to explain why recent administrations have preferred to have trusted top lieutenants conduct a version of national strategic planning in smaller, less formal, more ad hoc groups. The advantage of this approach, in addition to those already suggested, is that its results will reflect the collective wisdom, and presumably the consensus views, of those on whom the president has chosen to place the most reliance.

The disadvantages are twofold. First, top political appointees are likely to share many of the same assumptions and opinions, thereby increasing the risk of "groupthink." Second, because those people are extremely busy with other responsibilities, a planning process that depends on their participation is likely to be sporadic, partial, and unsystematic. It is very difficult to perform any of the functions listed above with a group of people small enough to fit in the White House Situation Room and virtually impossible to perform some of them when that group can meet together, at most, for forty-five-minute intervals one or two days a week.

Intellectual Predilections

If the relevant officials do not believe that improving the national strategic planning process is feasible or even desirable, the situation that exists today, and has existed with some minor variations since the early 1960s, is not going to change. The deepest obstacles to the creation of an effective planning mechanism lie in the minds of the people who would have to expend energy and political capital to bring it into existence.

Many of those who have had experience at high levels of government in recent years regard the notion of trying to create a national strategic planning process with a mix of bemusement and scorn. Some argue that such a mechanism already exists in the form of the process that produces annual national strategy statements. Others claim more plausibly that it is, and ought to be, embodied in the informal deliberations of the president and his inner circle. Finally, there are those who insist that they "do strategy" on an ongoing basis as part of a fluid, seamless process of deliberation and decisionmaking. Broader, more formal planning exercises, they say, are cumbersome, slow, prone to leaks, and likely to produce results that are bland, if not entirely devoid of serious content.

Not surprisingly, the attitudes and preferences of most of those who have risen through the contemporary national security system reflect the incentives it embodies. In this world, the most important people are usually those who are perceived to be most directly involved in the making and implementation of policy on the most pressing issues of the day. Such people are intensely busy with meetings, phone calls, and travel; their focus is on operations rather than planning and on tactics rather than strategy. Although they may recognize the importance of having a sense of strategic direction to guide their actions, for the most part they take strategy as a given. In any day, month, or year, a very small fraction of their time will be devoted to contemplating strategic issues.

Creating a Strategic Planning Capability

There are at least three ways in which the U.S. government's strategic planning capabilities could be strengthened. These are discussed here in descending order of potential payoff, but also of likely difficulty. Recreating something such as the Eisenhower-era Planning Board could have a substantial positive impact on U.S. strategic performance. Yet overcoming the predictable obstacles and objections in order to make it work would also demand a major investment of presidential time and energy. Restructuring the NSC to include a fully staffed planning directorate would pose fewer bureaucratic challenges, but there is a greater risk that its work would become decoupled from actual policy. Finally, although it is a relatively simple matter for an NSA to appoint one or two full-time planners, experience suggests that their contributions will necessarily be constrained by the limits on their own time and energy.

A New Planning Board

Eisenhower's Planning Board was made up of the top officials responsible for strategic planning from each relevant agency. In an indication of how important he considered it to be, the president gave the board members very specific instructions on how they were to approach their work. Among other things, they were prohibited from accompanying their bosses on international trips so that they could "stay on the job and supply a continuity of planning and thought," but were also expected to have "an unbreakable engagement" to brief their principals before each meeting of the full NSC.[6] Despite being deeply involved in the work of their home agencies, in their role as board members they were "to see themselves as part of a 'corporate body' whose responsibilities were to the president, not to their department or agencies." Eisenhower instructed members that they were to seek "statesman-like solutions to the problems of national security, rather than to reach solutions which represent merely a compromise of departmental positions."[7]

According to former Eisenhower administration official Robert Bowie and historian Richard Immerman, the board's function was to "analyze trends, anticipate as well as identify problems, consider proposed solutions' advantages and disadvantages, and [explicitly] confront . . . questions of means and ends." It was intended to be the mechanism through which "relevant expertise, intelligence data, and experience from the rest of the government" was drawn together and integrated. Members were expected to draw on the resources of their home agencies, but were also empowered to request "memoranda, staff studies, and other pertinent data" from all parts of the government.[8]

The Planning Board often convened two or more times each week, sometimes for as long as three hours at a stretch. Bowie and Immerman describe these meetings as "extremely intimate and informal" with the special assistant for national security affairs (still considered, at that time, primarily as a manager of the NSC system, rather than an adviser in his own right) in the chair, and nine or ten participants seated around a small table. The end products of these deliberations were policy papers that laid out issues and alternatives and often identified critical disagreements that remained to be resolved by the

NSC principals. These papers were briefed to principals before full NSC meetings and served to structure their deliberations.[9]

Because of the ways in which the national security system has evolved since the 1950s, this model would require a number of modifications to make it workable today. First, given the growth of the NSA's responsibilities for day-to-day policy, it is unrealistic to expect that he would be able to devote sufficient time to running an ongoing planning process. For this reason it might be advisable to appoint two deputy NSAs, one charged with assisting in the management of the policy process and the other with overseeing strategic planning.

Recreating something like the Eisenhower cross-governmental planning process would also require identifying an appropriate participant from each relevant agency. In some cases the identity of this person would be more obvious than in others. The Department of State's designee would presumably still be the director of the policy planning staff, just as it was in the 1950s. Officials with equivalent responsibilities would also be designated by the Office of the Secretary of Defense, the Joint Chiefs, and the intelligence community. To participate effectively and at an appropriate level in a government-wide process, some agencies might need to consolidate and strengthen their own departmental strategic planning capabilities and perhaps create new positions with responsibility for coordinating them and joining in interagency deliberations.

Compared to Eisenhower's day, there are now several additional layers of interagency committees and meetings below those of the full NSC chaired by the president. Among these are the Principals Committee, essentially the NSC minus the president, chaired by the national security adviser; the Deputies Committee, made up of the second in command to each of the principals, chaired by the deputy NSA; and an assortment of regional and functional Policy Coordinating Committees, generally made up of lower-ranking personnel from the relevant agencies and chaired by a member of the NSC staff. Feeding the products of a new planning process directly to the top of this pyramid would no longer be appropriate. One alternative would be to have a new planning board, perhaps reconstituted as a special NSC interagency Strategy Coordinating Committee, brief its reviews and recommendations to the Deputies Committee, which could then either request further refinements or approve the recommendations for consideration by the principals.

The main advantage of this approach is that, if it could be made to work, it would create a powerful mechanism for pooling the perspectives, and synchronizing the collective thought and action, of the entire executive branch. Balanced against this is the risk that, if not staffed with the right kinds of people and treated with sufficient seriousness at the highest levels, a formal interagency planning process would generate reams of bureaucratic pap rather than fresh strategic thought. Such a mechanism could also become bogged down in disputes that left it deadlocked or incapable of producing results that represented anything more than the lowest-common-denominator conventional wisdom as opposed to sharply defined alternatives. Barring some change in prevailing norms, a broad-based planning mechanism would probably also be more prone to leaks than one whose members were drawn exclusively from the NSC staff.[10]

An NSC Strategic Planning Directorate

A second, somewhat less ambitious approach would bypass the potential pitfalls and complications of trying to build a full-blown interagency planning process and focus instead on strengthening the capabilities of the NSC itself. One way of doing this would be to create an NSC strategic planning directorate equivalent in organizational status to offices that already exist to cover key regions and functional issues. Such an office, like others in the NSC structure, would have a staff made up of personnel seconded from relevant departments, as well as experts hired from business and academia. It would also have the authority to request information and analysis from other parts of the government and a budget to pay for studies by nongovernmental agencies.

The main function of an NSC planning directorate would be to assist the national security adviser in his or her efforts to support the president and to guide the formulation and implementation of national policy. The NSA might request a planning directorate to conduct an assessment of current strategy on a particular issue, to prepare a set of alternative approaches to a given problem, or to examine the possible implications of a critical contingency. A dedicated staff of planners could also assist the other NSC directorates in their work, helping them to add a strategic dimension to their efforts to manage current issues. Finally, to the extent that it had the necessary time and resources, a planning directorate could take the initiative in drawing attention to important trends or potential long-term issues.

Unlike an interagency board, an NSC directorate would have no direct access to or leverage over the thinking and planning of other parts of the government. Under this model, the flow of ideas would be primarily from the top down: from the NSC through the relevant agencies via principals, deputies, or the various policy-coordinating committees. Because of its size and composition, there is probably a better chance that an in-house NSC group would do work that is intellectually sharp and rigorous. Its analysis, however, would run the risk of having little impact, whether because of bureaucratic opposition, indifference, or the simple absence of effective follow-up mechanisms for ensuring that policy is actually driven by strategy.

An NSC Strategic Planning Cell

A third and final model would forgo the construction of a full-scale directorate and designate a small group of perhaps no more than two or three people to serve as strategic planning consultants to the NSA and perhaps also to the heads of the NSC directorates. This would essentially involve a continuation, and perhaps a modest expansion, of the unit established during the closing years of the Bush administration. An NSC cell would have the manpower to conduct its own analyses of only a handful of problems. For the most part, it would either review the work of others, commission internal or external analyses of questions of interest to the NSA, or assist in establishing and overseeing NSC-only or interagency working groups to ensure that they addressed core strategic questions.

Provided that it did not get caught up in more immediate business and assuming that it had the ear of the NSA, such a cell could help to raise the overall quality of the government's strategic thinking. Its impact, however, would inevitably be limited by its size and its weak, indirect connections to the rest of the bureaucracy.

Waiting for the Next Catalyst

In the U.S. system, major changes in the structure and functioning of the executive branch typically come in the wake of crises that sweep away the usual obstacles to innovation or in the immediate aftermath of elections that bring new presidents to power. In 1947, within a year of the clear collapse of relations with the Soviet Union, the Truman administration had called into being the NSC, the CIA, and most of the other mechanisms with which the United States would conduct the cold war. Six years later, with an eye on the difficult, long-term competition that he believed lay ahead, Eisenhower made significant adjustments to the structures he had inherited.

After September 11, 2001, the Bush administration rearranged large chunks of the federal bureaucracy, in the process creating several substantial new organizations such as the Department of Homeland Security and the Office of the Director of National Intelligence. Whatever the merits of these changes, they have done little, if anything, to enhance the nation's capacity for strategic thought and action. Such improvements are badly needed, but it will be up to President Obama to make them.

Notes

An earlier version of this chapter originally appeared in the *Washington Quarterly* 31 (Winter 2007/08), pp. 47–60.

1. Eisenhower, quoted in Richard Nixon, *Six Crises* (Garden City, N.J.: Doubleday, 1962), p. 235.

2. Dean Acheson, *Present at the Creation: My Years in the State Department* (New York: W. W. Norton, 1969), p. 214.

3. Michèle A. Flournoy and Shawn W. Brimley, "Strategic Planning for National Security: A New Project Solarium," *Joint Forces Quarterly* 41 (Spring 2006): 84.

4. See "The NSC at 50: Past, Present, and Future," Council on Foreign Relations, October 31, 1997 (www.cfr.org/publication/64/nsc_at_50.html [December 15, 2008]).

5. Ibid.

6. Quoted in Robert R. Bowie and Richard H. Immerman, *Waging Peace: How Eisenhower Shaped an Enduring Cold War Strategy* (Oxford University Press, 1998), pp. 91, 92.

7. Ibid., p. 91.

8. Ibid.

9. Ibid.

10. In August 2008, President Bush signed a National Security Policy Directive institutionalizing what had previously been an informal series of lunch meetings involving strategic planners from the NSC, the intelligence community, and other departments. This mechanism could provide the foundation for a stronger and more influential strategic planning process, if the Obama administration chooses to build one.

7

A Strategic Planning Cell on National Security at the White House

Any effort to do strategic planning on national security at the White House encounters a paradox. On the one hand, it is hard to do because even the largest White House feels understaffed and the time horizons of those staff are necessarily focused on dealing with the urgent tyranny of the president's daily "to do" list—the most daunting in-box in the U.S. government, perhaps in the world. Conversely, strategic planning on national security is hard to do anywhere besides the White House because the long-term fruits of strategic planning form such a central part of the president's vision and legacy, and only the president has the authority to cut across the various stove-piped interagency interests.

In its second term, the Bush administration sought to balance this unavoidable trade-off by creating a new strategic planning advisory cell on the National Security Council (NSC). We staffed and helped establish this office (Feaver as special adviser, and Inboden as senior director). Our efforts represented more activity in this area than the NSC had undertaken in the first term—and possibly in the previous administration—but the actions we took fell far short of some of the more dramatic recommendations circulating (including ones in this book). We encourage those who come after us to, at a minimum, continue using a strategic planning cell. We also propose a few ways to strengthen it.

What We Did

When Stephen Hadley succeeded Condoleezza Rice as national security adviser in 2005, he reorganized the NSC staff structure. Drawing on his own extensive national security experience as well as a careful review of previous organizational models for the NSC, Hadley perceived the need for a more deliberate and sophisticated approach to strategic planning. This led him to establish two new senior-level offices. The Strategic Planning and Institutional Reform (SPIR) cell was headed by a special adviser (Feaver, then Mary Habeck) and included one senior director (Inboden, then Paul Lettow) and a research assistant (initially Rebekah Rein, then Sarah Gelinas, and eventually Gillian Turner); this office reported directly to Stephen Hadley. A sister cell for Policy Implementation and Execution (PIE) was also headed by a special adviser (initially Susan Sweatt, then Lisa Disbrow, and eventually Anthony Harriman) and included one senior director (initially Disbrow, then Traci Sanders, and eventually John Tsagronis) and shared the research assistant. This office reported directly to the deputy NSA and focused initially on process reforms within the NSC; it eventually took over SPIR's "institutional reform" portfolio to look at broader interagency organizational issues.

Besides working directly for the NSA and DNSA, our cells worked closely with the other "line" offices of the NSC, the regional and functional directorates. We also worked closely with other White House offices devoted to general administration strategy.

SPIR's activities grouped into five broad baskets: cross-cutting, top-level strategy; longer-range analysis; internal critique; policy incubator; and outreach.

Cross-Cutting, Top-Level Strategy

SPIR's primary activity areas were any top-level strategy that involved multiple issues and cut across multiple NSC directorates (and therefore multiple departments and agencies) or that spread beyond the NSC to other White House offices. This gave SPIR one of the few issues it "owned," the drafting of the 2006 National Security Strategy (NSS). The administration responded to the Goldwater-Nichols mandate (the 1986 law that reorganized the Department of Defense and updated national security coordination) for an NSS by producing two editions, one for the first term (released in 2002) and one for the second term (released in 2006). At SPIR we received clear guidance from the president's articulation of his vision for the new NSS and then worked closely with NSA Hadley to draft a document that reflected that vision. In turn, we coordinated the review and editing of this document with a very small team of senior counterparts (at the major departments—State, Defense, and Treasury—and in the intelligence community) and vetted individual sections with every White House and NSC office with relevant equities. This process was designed to avoid the "written by committee" laundry list of policies that can beset such documents, undermining their coherence and clarity. Rather, in giving the NSS to one office, the president intended to produce a unified document that authoritatively articulated his strategic priorities across a range of issues and explained the strategic logic that integrated those priorities.

The NSS led to other internal planning efforts. We worked with the PIE cell to implement the guidance by developing specific objectives and targets that were directly linked to the strategy. PIE developed a management tool that allowed the NSC to track and evaluate the specific policy inputs, outputs, and outcomes that emanated from the National Security Strategy. Likewise, we worked with other offices to develop unclassified and classified strategy documents that derived from the strategic guidance laid out in the NSS, such as the update to the National Strategy for Combating Terrorism.

Some national security issues are so broad that they involve several NSC directorates. While one office might be designated a lead office, others have comparable equities. Especially when the issue was of high presidential priority, these were prime candidates for SPIR involvement. The effort to bolster the "war of ideas" component of the "global war on terror" is one example. Following the September 11 attacks, the Bush administration realized that America's militant Islamist enemies would need to be fought with the force of ideas as well as arms. But ascertaining exactly how to equip and engage in the "war of ideas" proved a persistent challenge. The prevailing national security structures were inadequate, and the origins, causes, and ideology of the foes were little understood. Into the second term, the administration had made progress on this front, but much remained to be done. SPIR played a key role in "war of ideas" task forces involving other NSC directorates as well as interagency representatives.

SPIR was a focal point at the White House for presidential priorities in the national security arena. In that capacity we worked closely with other White House offices that were similarly oriented to top, presidential-level priorities across the policy spectrum: the senior adviser (Karl Rove) and especially his director of the Office of Strategic Initiatives (Pete Wehner); the assistant to the president for policy and strategic planning (Michael Gerson); and the counselor to the president (Dan Bartlett). The president's chief of staff viewed SPIR, in partnership with these other offices, as something of an in-house think tank to be tasked with analyses and reviews that were too sensitive to be done outside the White House.

The budget integration function, which many proposals have linked to strategic planning and so would be a logical SPIR assignment, was handled within the NSC by the other special adviser's office (PIE) in support of the Directorate for Relief, Stabilization, and Development. SPIR worked with PIE to identify presidential priorities and to advise the national security adviser on budget items requiring his personal attention.

SPIR worked closely with the strategic planning offices at the Department of State (chiefly the director of policy planning, Steve Krasner, and then David Gordon) and at the Department of Defense (chiefly the deputy assistant secretary of defense for policy planning, Thomas Mahnken). This began as informal regular lunches and over time evolved into a more formal interagency working group that included representatives from the National Intelligence Council.

Longer-Range, Deeper-Look, and Retrospective Studies

SPIR was also the natural home for designing, commissioning, and in some cases conducting special analyses devoted to topics of presidential interest. Sometimes these stayed within the NSC and took the form of "deeper dives," looking in depth at an issue of current or looming concern. In these cases, SPIR would work with the relevant directorate to draft a paper outlining the issue and then convene a small group of NSC staff for a series of brainstorming discussions led by the national security adviser. Topics explored in these sessions included the future of Asian regional architecture, democracy promotion, Western Hemisphere trends, public diplomacy, and reviewing strategies for transitioning countries such as Pakistan and Russia. On some occasions, these sessions led to specific presidential initiatives, and at other times the discussions served to reinforce existing policy lines.

SPIR also oversaw the production of studies that involved the interagency taking a longer-horizon exploration of a particular country or issue beyond the range of typical intelligence products. The SPIR office initiated these studies, worked with other NSC offices to draft outlines of the terms of reference, and then shared the outlines with senior officials at State, Defense, the Joint Chiefs of Staff, and Treasury and in the intelligence community. Once the relevant officials provided their feedback in further shaping the terms of reference, the National Intelligence Council took the lead on coordinating production of the studies. This process ensured not only that the particular insights and concerns of different departments and agencies were incorporated, but also that the final studies would command attention—and where appropriate, action—across agency boundaries.

The standard, clichéd-but-true rationale for establishing a discrete strategic planning office is the need to escape the day-to-day tyranny of the in-box and look "over the horizon" at potential threats, challenges, and opportunities. Valid though this aim is, it neglects another unique dimension of a distinct strategic planning office: the capacity to also look back, into the past, for insights into the challenges of the present day. For SPIR, excavating history became a regular responsibility.

The methodological foundation of these exercises in strategic history does not presume that the answers to present and future challenges are to be found in simply avoiding (or replicating) the failed (or successful) actions of the past. In other words, it is not enough to just say, "Don't fight land wars in Asia." Rather, the use of history in strategic planning is complex, nuanced, and precarious. Sometimes history functions as a cautionary tale, showing the myriad and unexpected ways in which policy lines may be insufficient or ineffective. At other times history can illumine the art of the possible, demonstrating that the conventional limitations, assumptions, or prejudices of the day are not valid, just as they were not in the past. History can also provide perspective, broadening the scope through which policies are assessed, taking into account the passage of time and second- and third-order effects. And history can be an encouragement, providing a buffer from the contentions of the incessant political and media cycles that threaten to overwhelm sound policymaking.

To help inform current policymaking, the SPIR office produced short studies on topics as varied as the histories of counterinsurgency campaigns, Iranian hostage-taking, organizational models for ideological warfare, executive-congressional relations during the Vietnam War, and institution building during the early cold war years. At other times, this use of history led to a specific presidential action, such as President Bush's 2007 speech at the Washington Islamic Center, which also marked the fiftieth anniversary of President Eisenhower's dedication of the center. Though separated by a half-century and different geopolitical environments, both presidential visits represented efforts to enlist and support peaceful Islamic leaders in global ideological struggles, whether against atheistic communism or violent jihadism.

Internal Critiques

A significant portion of SPIR's analytic focus concerned what may best be called second-guessing existing policy lines. These would often take the form of highly classified memos designed for a very limited distribution that assessed problems with existing policies and opportunities for change. On a few occasions, the results would emerge into public view. Thus, working very closely with the NSC's Iraq directorate, SPIR was involved at the inception of what later morphed into the Iraq Strategy Review of late fall 2006—the internal reexamination of our Iraq strategy that resulted in the New Way Forward announced by President Bush on January 10, 2007 (popularly known as "the surge"). SPIR was involved in other exercises, some of which resulted in policy changes and others that served to confirm that existing policies, while perhaps imperfect, were nevertheless the most plausible among a challenging range of options.

SPIR led a similar process for certain kinds of contingency planning. Intended both to diagnose possible vulnerabilities in policy lines and to prepare for possible "strategic shocks" to the national security system, these studies considered initial responses for a series of "what if" crisis scenarios. As with the country studies described above, the contingency planning studies involved senior interagency representatives throughout, from developing the scenarios to drafting the response plans. It is perhaps a grim commentary on the gravity of the exercise that more than one of these contingencies actually came to pass during the process.

One final SPIR activity in this basket involved helping the NSC leadership with internal NSC concerns. The NSC staff's core function is to manage the interagency process and resolve interagency disputes at as low a level as possible, playing an honest-broker role (but with an eye to presidential priorities) and then bringing up to the deputy (or higher) level only those issues requiring, and ripe for, senior decision. Some issues, however, produced intra-NSC staff disputes, and in some cases SPIR helped play the same honest-broker role within the NSC staff that the NSC staff played within the interagency process. Just as the NSC staff serves as the president's early warning radar into interagency coordination, so SPIR served as the national security adviser's early warning radar on NSC staff coordination.

Policy Incubator

The National Security Strategy established the priorities and parameters that would govern the administration's second-term policies. Although SPIR was not responsible for implementing the strategy, it was responsible for helping ensure its implementation. This sometimes entailed developing and incubating new policy initiatives, particularly in areas that intersected with multiple regional or functional directorates and were otherwise not being sufficiently advanced. This also meant serving as the designated clearinghouse for "forum shopping" by outsiders (or insiders) who had policy proposals that they sought to inject into (or elevate within) the policymaking process.

One SPIR initiative that embodied many of these dynamics was the Asia-Pacific Democracy Partnership (APDP). The APDP originated as a vehicle to address several needs, including bolstering Asia's relatively weak regional architecture, enlisting partner nations in the effort to promote democratic governance, building multilateral organizations focused on action and results, and institutionalizing the NSS's emphasis on promoting "effective democracy."

Because the NSC in general and SPIR in particular do not have a mandate to be operational, any new initiatives needed to be linked with the relevant interagency officials and offices that would be responsible for implementation. This was no simple task. It is almost axiomatic that the default setting of departments and agencies is to resist new initiatives. The reasons are several, and include suspicion that the new initiative represents a judgment that the policy is not already being carried out (or else why the need for a new initiative?), concern that the new project merely duplicates existing initiatives, indifference toward or even resentment of any idea "not invented here," and the fatigue and frustration that stems from limited resources and expanding responsibilities.

To advance the APDP, SPIR drafted a strategic plan, secured support from other NSC directorates and the national security adviser, and convened several meetings to seek input from representatives of relevant bureaus and offices at State, Defense, and the U.S. Agency for International Development (USAID). Policy Planning Director Steve Krasner and his staff at the State Department played a particularly active and helpful role. Having achieved interagency consensus, SPIR partnered with Under Secretary of State for Democracy and Global Affairs Paula Dobriansky and her staff to negotiate support from other democratic nations in the region. These efforts culminated in President Bush's announcement of the APDP in September 2007 at the Asia-Pacific Economic Cooperation (APEC) conference in Sydney.

Since then, thirteen Asia-Pacific democracies have agreed to participate in the APDP. Mongolia hosted an inaugural planning meeting in July 2008, and Japan provided substantial funding for the APDP's inaugural election monitoring missions to observe the Mongolian parliamentary elections. In October 2008, South Korea hosted a meeting of senior officials to further develop regional strategy, establish operational procedures, and select future projects.

SPIR also helped to shepherd new initiatives developed in other planning offices through the interagency process and toward approval and implementation. For example, Steve Krasner and the State Department's policy planning staff designed the Partnership for Democratic Governance (PDG). Intended to address the "governance gap" by assisting nations that have political will but little capacity in the provision of specific government services, the PDG filled an important lane in a comprehensive democracy promotion strategy. SPIR worked with the policy planning staff to help secure NSC and interagency support for the PDG, which under Secretary of State Rice's leadership was launched by the OECD and UNDP at the United Nations General Assembly in 2007. Twelve countries and international organizations were founding members of the PDG, and its Advisory Unit is housed at the OECD in Paris, headed by a Polish diplomat with a small staff. The PDG is currently in dialogue with several developing countries interested in its assistance and began pilot programs in October 2008.

Outreach

Stephen Hadley endorsed the mantra "in-source inspiration and out-source perspiration." A crucial part of SPIR's mandate was to utilize more effectively the vast intellectual resources in the private sector that were devoted to the same issues that we were working on inside government. In some cases, they were developing the same policy ideas we were developing and could become natural allies in the politics of policymaking. In other cases, they proposed in richer detail and nuance ideas that we were weighing and so could make timely interventions into decisionmaking. And in some instances they proposed alternatives that constituted the "best case against what we wanted to do," and so were vital sounding boards. Sometimes they had analytical expertise and, more valuably, time to devote to the problem and so could be leveraged and applied to challenges and opportunities we had yet to resolve. And, finally, in certain cases, outsiders had precisely the mix of insight and objectivity necessary to help the president think through a specific policy problem. A core mission for SPIR was identifying good matches between insider national security policy needs and outsider national security policy offers.

The liaison work integral to this matching process lent itself naturally to outreach across the political spectrum. Thus SPIR was in close contact with outside experts and institutions ranging from the president's most conservative supporters (and critics) to a panoply of the "loyal opposition." A bitter partisan climate characterized national security policy in the later years of the Bush administration, and it was SPIR's explicit mandate to cut against those tendencies, where possible. Within the administration, Stephen Hadley possessed unique credibility across the partisan aisle and so played a major role in forging whatever bipartisan support was available. On certain key issues, SPIR had that file for the NSC.

This role gave SPIR a front-row seat to the evolving critiques of administration policy. Part of our job, therefore, was to understand those critiques, to bring inside those critiques that had merit, and to refine our rebuttal for those that did not. For this reason, we helped the communicators and press teams at the White House to craft persuasive explanations of our policies—essentially, the task of strategic messaging. This, in turn, meant that we were given more latitude for both speaking in public and providing background to the press than the typical NSC office in the Bush administration enjoyed.

What We Learned

Our experience reaffirmed many strategic planning truisms and afforded some new lessons as well. These include:

Just because it is a cliché doesn't mean it isn't true. Strategic planners love the aphorism "It's not the plan but the planning," which our experience further validated. Although several of our initiatives, including planning sessions, studies, and "second-look" memos either posited scenarios that never came to pass or never resulted in concrete action, the very process of doing them enhanced the NSC's strategic outlook and helped prepare Hadley and other White House principals to respond better to other contingencies when they did arise.

The primacy of personality. Because we did not control a budget or policy lane on any particular issue or region, our ability to function effectively depended in large part on having the trust and esteem of the line directorates. We had to demonstrate to them up front that we were honest, discreet, and collegial and that we could add value to their work. To a certain degree, within the NSC, SPIR had to overcome the old joke, "Hello, we are here from the government and we want to help you." Having good ideas to offer was necessary but not sufficient; of equal importance was a willingness to defer credit to the line directorates, divert blame to ours, and above all work collaboratively and with goodwill.

The power of propinquity. We could function only if our fellow NSC staff and interagency colleagues perceived that we were trusted by and had independent access to the national security adviser and other White House principals. Fortunately, we did enjoy such trust and access. This infused a sense of consequence and purpose into our efforts, and increased our influence. It also helped enormously to have relatively unstructured access in the form of regular Saturday planning meetings with NSA Hadley, sometimes with a fixed agenda and sometimes devoted to more free-flowing discussion of strategic issues.

The power of the pen. Beyond our independent access to the NSA and White House principals, a key driver of our effectiveness was owning at least one unavoidable lane: the National Security Strategy. Strategic planners everywhere in the government have to vie with line officers for relevance to policymaking, and this obtained at the NSC too. By having the pen for the top-line strategy document in the government, we were relevant whether or not they wanted us to be.

A restrained partisanship. Given our mandate to help define and defend the president's national security policies, our partisan convictions had to be robust enough to warrant the trust of the rest of the White House political and communications offices. However, we had to be independent enough to be respected by the career professionals of the NSC staff and interagency—and willing to resign (or be fired) if conscience determined that our party was irreparably wrong.

"Multilingual" interagency communication. Just like the other NSC directorates, SPIR needed to speak the language and navigate the landscape of the various departments and agencies, especially State and Defense. This meant staffing SPIR with people who had knowledge of and access to both Defense (Feaver) and State (Inboden). Our successors, Mary Habeck and Paul Lettow, continued this model. The PIE office also followed it, being staffed by officials from Defense (Sweatt/Disbrow/Harriman), Treasury (Sanders), and State/USAID (Tsagronis).

Long-term perspective, short-term relevance. Since anything involving the president is by definition "important," the old urgent vs. important strategic planning trade-off is experienced at the White House as urgent importance vs. not urgent importance. To be effective in such an environment, we had to be relevant to the short term and, in particular, to have fairly wide situational awareness of urgent operations, even lines that we were not working ourselves. As one colleague put it, we were not responsible for firing at guerrillas in the wire (the normal NSC staffer job), but we had to be aware of where they were and when there were opportunities for a strategically timed intervention. The countervailing challenge, of course, was not to become so operationally involved in current policies that we had no time free to do the step-back assessment work of strategic planning.

It's worse than that. The besetting sin of designated second-guessers is only identifying problems with existing policies and not identifying solutions. Indeed, it is much easier to see challenges than it is to see opportunities. One colleague joked that the mantra of SPIR could be "It's worse than that" because our internal critiques could be quite pointed. We had to thread the needle between adding independent value and simply being viewed as cranky contrarians.

Choose your battles. We faced the constant challenge of staying abreast of several disparate issues while not getting spread too thin trying to address every last issue facing the NSC. This meant choosing our engagements strategically, based on the priority of the issue, our own expertise, and the needs of the NSA and other directorates.

Set the agenda. Another balance we had to maintain was between being responsive to taskings from the national security adviser and independently bringing "uninvited" issues or initiatives to his attention. We could not disregard the former, but we also believe we served him and the president best by taking the initiative to offer unsolicited cautions, assessments, and opportunities.

What We Recommend for the Next Team

The administration of Barack Obama will likely rearrange the NSC organization chart, if only to mark the territory as belonging to the new team. However, we strongly recommend that in the midst of reorganizing, some sort of independent strategic planning cell be maintained within the NSC and that it be augmented. We believe that our efforts represented some progress, a progress that is worth preserving and improving on.

In order to improve on what we did, we recommend that the next team embrace the lessons we learned (outlined above) and consider the following additional changes:

Add staff. Even by the comparatively minimal staffing levels of the NSC, a two-person cell is quite small and inherently limited in the impact it can have. Adding one or two directors could have a significant multiplier effect on the office's reach and effectiveness.

Tighten the link to resources. The NSC has an established process of coordinating with the Office of Management and Budget (OMB) on budget priorities. This process can be effective at preserving important presidential initiatives and adjudicating between a few competing priorities. However, numerous outside observers have noted a discrepancy between overall strategic objectives and overall resource allocations. Having a small sub-cell devoted to evaluating that balance and empowered to intervene (perhaps by co-staffing White House budget review meetings with OMB) would help strengthen the integration of resources and policies.

Further institutionalize interagency strategic planning. The offices with strategic planning portfolios at the key departments should meet regularly and, on a few critical topics, even staff certain projects that are worked up through the different tiers of the NSC's interagency coordination system. The National Security Policy Directive issued by President Bush in August 2008 setting up a National Security Policy Planning Committee (NSPPC) represents a positive step in this regard. Charged with coordinating planning efforts across agencies, the NSPPC's participants include senior officials responsible for strategic planning at the NSC, the Departments of State, Defense, Justice, and Treasury, the Joint Staff, and in the intelligence community.

Further empower the office within the White House. Ensuring effective communication and coordination between the NSC and the White House is a perennial challenge. The three officers with line responsibility for that function—the NSA, the DNSA, and the executive secretary of the NSC—all carry burdensome portfolios that can interfere with time-consuming intra–White House coordination. The strategic planning cell is a good point of contact because of its bird's eye perch and so could be empowered to fill that role on a more regular basis with a backseat at all relevant White House meetings.

A Parting Reflection

It is a special privilege to serve our nation in such a post in ordinary times. In times of war and grave national challenge, it is all the more extraordinary. No one working in such a position could help but respect the dedication, hard work, patriotism, and good sense of our colleagues and our leaders. The rancor that has too often characterized national security policy debates in the broader political environment could have a corrosive effect on the ideals of national service. But the animating spirit for strategic planning at the NSC, and the very principle of national security service, perhaps is best captured by a comment that President Bush once made in directing our office to conduct a particular study. Describing its purpose, he said that he wanted us to "consider what type of policy we should adopt now, which will lead my successor's successor in 2012 or 2016 to look back with appreciation." This perspective, we hope, inspired many of our efforts. And we hope that it will inspire the efforts of our successors as well.

PART
IV

Limits and Opportunities
for Strategic Planning

AMY B. ZEGART

8

Why the Best Is Not Yet to Come in Policy Planning

Policy planning is hard and getting harder. Created at the dawn of the cold war, the State Department's policy planning staff was designed to bring the future into the present—fusing longer-range, big-picture thinking with the here and now of U.S. foreign policymaking. Although some staffs have fared better than others, all have confronted four types of constraints: time pressures to address current issues at the expense of longer-term planning; bureaucratic competition for influence; cognitive barriers to anticipating the future; and cultural tensions between policy planning "thinkers" and policy-making "doers" within the U.S. government. All of these constraints have grown considerably worse since the cold war's end, suggesting that policy planning is likely to be more difficult in the twenty-first century than it was in the twentieth.

Variance Is Overrated

According to conventional wisdom, the policy planning staff's influence has fluctuated naturally—and sometimes wildly—across presidential administrations. For any particular staff, success hinges on three factors: the secretary of state's stature and personal relationship with the president; the policy planning staff director's rapport with the secretary; and the strategic demands of international politics writ large. When the connections between key players are close and trusted, and when the political moment demands rethinking foreign policy relationships and issues rather than managing the status quo, the planning staff prospers. When any one of these ingredients is missing, it struggles.

Like most pieces of conventional wisdom, this one captures part of reality, but not the most important part. For starters, history suggests that at least one of the key ingredients for success is often missing. Almost every president since Kennedy has relied more on his national security adviser and the National Security Council (NSC) staff than on the State Department.[1] Interpersonal relationships between secretaries of state and their policy planning staff directors have at times been distant, problematic, or both.[2] And the constancy and length of the cold war left little room for the kinds of dramatic conceptual breakthroughs that marked the policy planning staff's early days, when George Kennan and a handful of others laid the foundations for the Marshall Plan and the doctrine of containment. When the golden days of policy planning are half a century old, something more systematic is probably at work.

Organization theory also suggests that variance is not the whole story. Sure, staffs differ. But the real question is how much. The policy planning staff's success is not entirely up for grabs each inauguration day. Instead, the staff, like all organizations, is bounded or constrained by a broader set of forces that organization theorists have been studying for years. They find that the key drivers of organizational success often lurk in the background, in the silent ways that people process information,[3] seek career advancement,[4] and interact with the organization's culture, among others.[5] This is a long way away from the personality clashes and policy debates that make headlines and form the basis of popular perspectives. As former CIA Director Michael Hayden warned during his 2006 confirmation hearings, what you find often depends on what you seek. "I got three great kids," Hayden told the Senate Intelligence Committee, "but if you tell me, 'Go out and find all the bad things they've done, Hayden,' I could build you a pretty good dossier, and you'd think they were pretty bad people, because that was what I was looking for and that's what I'd built up."[6] The same is true of policy planning. Seeking variance, observers find it. In the end, however, forces transcending individual personalities may matter more.

Finally, "it-depends-on-the-people" explanations offer juicy nuance but little predictive power. Of course, hollow generalities are not of much help either. The trick is to find the middle ground that lies between the granularity of the real world and the distant blur of theory. Identifying what makes all policy planning staffs alike rather than what makes them different is a good place to start. Here I examine the temporal, bureaucratic, cognitive, and cultural constraints that have hindered every policy planning staff, and what these constraints mean for the future.

The "Thundering Present"

The first challenge that all policy planning staffs face is temporal. What Secretary of State Dean Acheson called the "thundering present" has exerted tremendous pressure on secretaries of state to focus on current issues at the expense of longer-term planning.[7] This is not intentional. Although senior policymakers across the U.S. foreign policy establishment have long expressed the desire for strategic planning and "over-the-horizon" thinking, putting aside the talent and time has been quite another matter. As Acheson noted, day-to-day problems typically consume the State Department's energies even though "the true problem lies in determining the emerging future and the policy appropriate to it."[8]

Ironically, it was the specter of looming catastrophe that led to the creation of the State Department's policy planning unit in the first place. In his memoirs, Kennan recalls that on April 28, 1947, Secretary of State George Marshall returned from a meeting of the Council of Foreign Ministers in Moscow "shaken" by the "realization of the seriousness and urgency of the plight of Western Europe," where economic collapse appeared imminent.[9] The very next day, Marshall summoned Kennan to his office and instructed him to set up a policy planning staff without delay. "Europe was in a mess. Something would have to be done," Kennan wrote.[10] The new director had no staff, no office, and just two weeks to examine the complex economic and political issues of European economic recovery in the context of the Soviet communist threat and present his recommendations to Secretary Marshall.[11] The State Department's premier longer-range planning unit was born a creature of crisis.

Twenty years later, Henry Kissinger was still lamenting that top State Department officials were too distracted by answering the thousands of cables they received each day to think ahead. "Planning," he wrote, "involves conjectures about the future and hypothetical cases." But top officials "are so busy with actual cases that they are reluctant to take on theoretical ones."[12] Kissinger advised any foreign government interested in influencing American foreign policy to focus on the assistant secretary level because "that is the highest level in which people can still think" without getting overtaken by the "day to day operation of the machine."[13] Foggy Bottom is not alone. The National Security Council staff, the Defense Department, the Central Intelligence Agency, and the rest of the U.S. intelligence community have been battling in-box overload for years. As the old saying goes in Washington, the urgent too often crowds out the important.

Since the cold war's end, the drumbeat of policymaking has grown substantially faster and louder. The rapid spread of the Internet and cell phones, the rise of BlackBerries and instant messaging, and the constant stream of news coming from twenty-four-hour cable, bloggers, and even YouTube—are all dramatically compressing the speed at which foreign policy decisions are made. Consider, for example, two snapshots of crisis decisionmaking. In 1962, President Kennedy and his aides spent thirteen days deliberating secretly about how the United States would respond to the Soviet Union's clandestine nuclear missile buildup in Cuba. Nearly forty years later, President George W. Bush and his aides had thirteen *hours* to respond to the 9/11 attacks that were being carried live on national television. Although many factors undoubtedly contributed to the peaceful end of the Cuban missile crisis, time to think was almost certainly one of them. Transcripts show that had Kennedy been forced to respond to the crisis on the first day, the United States would have launched an air strike to take out the missiles—a reaction that stood a much higher chance of triggering nuclear war than the less provocative naval blockade the president ultimately chose.[14]

The information revolution has made time to think harder to find, even on normal days. Planning efforts across the U.S. government are straining to deal with information flows that are unprecedented in both speed and scale. Today more than a billion people, or 20 percent of the world's population, are online,[15] including an increasingly sophisticated network of jihadists who use the Internet for recruiting, planning, operations, and propaganda.[16] The fastest growth in Internet use is happening in the world's most volatile region: the Middle East.[17] Half the people on earth now own cell phones and are finding new ways to use them—from banking in rural Africa[18] to organizing protests in urban China.[19]

With so much information being transmitted so quickly, taking the longer view has become more important but less likely. As the Weapons of Mass Destruction (WMD) Commission chaired by Judge Laurence Silberman and former senator Charles Robb warned in 2005, "The Intelligence Community we have today is buried beneath an avalanche of demands for 'current intelligence.'"[20] Former CIA Director Michael Hayden echoed this concern. "We must set aside talent and energy to look at the long view and not just be chasing our version of the current news cycle," Hayden warned in 2006, or else the United States would be "endlessly surprised." He bluntly told the Senate Intelligence Committee that this would not be easy. "I actually think it might be worse now than it has been historically," he said, noting that the twenty-four-hour news cycle and operations tempo in Afghanistan, Iraq, and the war on terror had "suck[ed] energy into doing something into the here and now."[21]

Turf

The second enduring constraint on policy planning involves the worst four-letter word in Washington: turf. The bureaucracy's natural penchant for self-protection is nothing new. In the 1940s, the Navy deliberately hobbled the Joint Chiefs of Staff (JCS) with unanimous voting rules and statutory prohibitions to ensure that Army and Air Force officials would have little say over Navy budget decisions, policies, or operations. As a result, the JCS coordination system remained dysfunctional for the next forty years.[22] In 1992, 1996, and 2004, Pentagon officials savaged intelligence reform bills that tried to create a powerful new national intelligence director because they threatened the Defense Department's control over several major intelligence agencies and the lion's share of the intelligence budget. The first two bills went down to defeat. Although the 2004 bill passed, the director of national intelligence it established has been roundly criticized as lacking budgetary and personnel authorities to knock bureaucratic heads together.[23]

The State Department's policy planning staff has always had a tougher time than most because it has to wage a two-front war—battling the regional and functional bureaus inside the building for influence with the secretary; and competing with the National Security Council staff, the Defense Department, and other bureaucratic players outside the building for influence with the president.

These bureaucratic turf issues explain a great deal about the policy planning staff's historical trajectory. It is no coincidence that policy planning's halcyon days came early. When the staff was created on May 5, 1947, regional bureaus reigned supreme, leaving few internal competitors to consider cross-cutting issues. Even more important, powerful external competitors did not yet exist. The National Security Council, NSC staff, Defense Department, and Central Intelligence Agency were not established until several months later, with the passage of the National Security Act of 1947. Even then, the NSC and its staff were largely ignored by President Truman, who feared encroachment on presidential foreign policy prerogatives. The Defense Department and Joint Chiefs of Staff were busy trying to integrate the old Navy and War Departments into a coherent whole. And the CIA was struggling to overcome its statutory defects, which gave the agency responsibility but little authority to actually centralize intelligence. In short, there was plenty of strategic think-ing to do and few bureaucratic players strong enough to do it.[24]

Over time, however, as these agencies matured and others emerged, the for-tunes of the State Department and its policy planning staff declined. By the time Lyndon Johnson took office, many of the department's responsibilities were already being eroded. The Departments of Treasury and Commerce assumed many international economic functions. A new White House agency, the Office of the Special Trade Representative (and the precursor to the Office of the U.S. Trade Representative), was created by executive order to handle international trade.[25] After the Bay of Pigs, Kennedy transformed his NSC staff from a paper-shuffling secretariat to a personal policy shop with offices both in the West Wing of the White House and in the Old Executive Office Building next door, making it a powerful rival for policy formulation. Although the policy planning staff has seen periods of resurgence (notably under Secretary of State Henry Kissinger, who immodestly called his policy planning staff "the most creative since the days of George Kennan,"[26] and under James Baker), the trajectory has been downhill.

The cold war's end accelerated and exacerbated these trends. Inside Foggy Bottom, the Soviet Union's collapse led to a proliferation of functional bureaus, ambassadors-at-large, special coordinators, and other new arrange-ments to deal with an increasingly complex array of transnational issues.[27] By 2001, the Hart-Rudman Commission found that a humanitarian disaster in Africa would fall under the purview of three under secretaries of state (for global affairs, political affairs, and international security affairs), and four bureaus (Africa; Democracy, Human Rights and Labor; Population, Refugees, and Migration; and Political-Military Affairs).[28]

Presidents, for their part, have increasingly outsourced big-picture think-ing in foreign affairs to blue-ribbon commissions. Between the Soviet Union's fall in 1991 and the terrorist attacks of 2001, presidents created forty-eight for-eign policy commissions. In contrast to domestic policy commissions, which are typically used to deflect blame or galvanize public support, the vast major-ity (68 percent) of these foreign policy commissions were used to generate ideas, facts, and analyses about key issues inside the government and away from the public eye—exactly the same kinds of analysis the policy planning staff is supposed to perform.[29] Between 1999 and 2001, for example, four dif-ferent bipartisan commissions issued major reports on terrorism and home-land security.[30] More recent commissions have assumed particularly public profiles in an effort to market their recommendations. While the Deutch,

Gilmore, and Bremer Commissions may not be household names, the 9/11 Commission, the WMD Commission, and the Iraq Study Group probably are. Indeed, during the summer of 2004, the 9/11 Commission received more television news coverage than the war in Iraq.[31]

The September 11, 2001, terrorist attacks triggered a frenzy of agency creation that produced the behemoth Department of Homeland Security, the Office of the Director of National Intelligence, the National Counterterrorism Center, the FBI's National Security Branch, and the Homeland Security Council in the White House. All have a hand in U.S. foreign policy and all consider elements of policy planning to be part of their mission. And that's just the federal government. In the post-9/11 world, national security is no longer just Washington's problem. Today there are more than fifty intelligence "fusion centers" around the country, in places as far-flung as Fort Harrison, Montana, and Bismarck, North Dakota.[32] The New York and Los Angeles police departments have their own intelligence analysis units. The New Jersey Office of Homeland Security has roughly two dozen analysts dedicated to strategic counterterrorism analysis. The Los Angeles County sheriff's department forward-deploys personnel abroad to enhance its counterterrorism efforts.

Although these organizations perform a wide range of functions, all of them are making policy planning more competitive, coherence more elusive, and coordination more difficult. George Kennan's observations on the perils of proliferating agencies are prescient. Testifying before the Senate in 1960, he noted:

> Even if we had the most excellent conceptual foundation for an American foreign policy and the greatest mastery of diplomatic method in our external relations, I feel we would still find ourselves seriously hampered, as things stand today, by the cumbersomeness of our governmental machinery. . . . The appalling growth in the numbers of personnel and the seemingly endless proliferation of competing agencies and committees has appeared to me to be only in minor part a response to real needs and in major part the result of some unhealthy internal compulsions, the source of which no one has as yet fully identified and the cure for which has certainly not yet been found.[33]

In short, while all policy planning staffs have contended with bureaucratic competition, recent developments suggest that these turf constraints are getting worse.

Cognitive Limits

The third challenge lies not in the world of technology or the halls of bureaucracy, but inside the human brain. Dean Acheson once described the essence of policy planning as "look[ing] ahead, not into the distant future, but beyond the vision of the operating officers caught in the smoke and crises of current battle; far enough ahead to see the emerging form of things to come and outline what should be done to meet or anticipate them."[34] But assessing the "emerging form of things to come" often requires analysts to think in ways they are not hardwired to do well. As Robert Jervis, Daniel Kahneman, and Amos Tversky have noted, individuals cope with uncertainty and incomplete information by using mental decisionmaking shortcuts that often lead them astray.[35] Cognitive traps are everywhere. People unconsciously select new information that confirms their hypotheses while discounting or ignoring information that does not. They assume the likelihood of future events based on the ease with which they recall similar examples. They have a hard time noticing Sherlock Holmes's dog that does not bark—in other words, the non-events, missing information, or possible outcomes that have not yet occurred. As Thomas Schelling put it, "There is a tendency in our planning to confuse the unfamiliar with the improbable."[36] In some ways, experts may be particularly disadvantaged because they are trained to think in terms of "normal theory" or likely events when unusual probabilities may be more important.[37] This might explain why foreign policy experts have been so historically bad at prediction.[38] In foreign policy, as in medicine, it is the rare case, not the typical one, that often proves disastrous.

It is fair to assume that avoiding cognitive traps will probably be more difficult in the future than in the past because analysts will have to cope with more information, increasing complexity, greater uncertainty, and an accelerating pace of change. When George Kennan led the policy planning staff, records were kept on paper, not computers. Today the National Security Agency intercepts 24 million faxes, e-mails, phone calls, and other signals every hour. That's 200 million pieces of information in a regular workday.[39] Globalization, the erosion of the state, and the rise of transnational threats from climate change to terrorism have dramatically increased the multidimensionality of foreign policy relationships and issues. The pace of technological change has also accelerated the development of unintended and unanticipated consequences. To give just one example, after the cell phone was invented in 1973, it took twenty years to get the first billion subscribers. It took four years to reach the second billion, and just two years to reach 3 billion.[40] The increasing speed of technological change has the potential for profound social, cultural, and political consequences, enabling ideas or movements to "go viral" faster than governments can respond. For policy planners, these developments mean that contingency planning will be more difficult because contingencies will be more numerous.

Culture

The fourth constraint rests in the inherent cultural conflicts between policy planners and policymakers. Policy planning staffers are analysts at heart. They are thinkers who sit apart from the hustle and bustle of the daily grind to consider future scenarios and options. They cannot be oblivious to the here and now, but to do their jobs well they must not be consumed by it either. Patience and longer-term perspectives are virtues. These inclinations are reinforced by a salient practical concern: to implement anything, policy planning staffers must enlist the support of the State Department's permanent bureaucracy, which is inevitably drawn to stability and incrementalism.

Policymakers are very different animals. They are doers, not thinkers, men and women of action, people who want to make a mark on the world and a legacy for the president's administration. The bureaucracy seeks to manage problems; political principals seek to solve them.

This cultural tension can be productive. But it can also lead to stalemate, policy blunders, and frustration. One crucial factor is whether the thinkers and doers agree on first principles, whether they see eye to eye about the basic contours of American grand strategy and American national interests. When they do, the odds in favor of policy coherence and policy success are higher.

During the cold war, first principles—containing the Soviet Union—were clear and long-lasting. That is no longer true. Is the core challenge of the next century to manage American decline or assert American power? Should the United States seek stability or transformation of the world order? Should American foreign policy be guided by national values or national interests? These questions have been percolating ever since the Soviet Union collapsed. While every administration has grappled with them, none has found a clear way forward. The Clinton administration embraced democratization and the assertive promotion of human rights before failed humanitarian interventions in Somalia and Haiti, China's economic rise, and North Korea's nuclear weapons program led to a more interest-based approach. Conversely, the Bush administration began with a realist-centered strategy, concentrating on great-power rivals and protecting vital American interests, but after 9/11 seized on regime change in Iraq and democratization in the Middle East as a bulwark against what they came to see as an existential terrorist threat. The uneasy drift between interests and values, institutions and unilateralism, and stability and change continues, with no end in sight. So long as the big questions remain unsettled, policy planning and policymaking will be hard to reconcile.

Conclusion

Yogi Berra rightly cautioned that predicting is hard, especially about the future. It could be that policy planning will enjoy more success in this century than in the previous one. But I doubt it. Personal relationships and favorable strategic opportunities are necessary but not sufficient conditions for good policy planning. Even if President Barack Obama gives the secretary of state unfettered leadership in foreign affairs, even if the policy planning director has the ear of the secretary and a nose for smart analysis, and even if the strategic landscape is conducive to big ideas and longer-term planning, the policy planning staff will have to confront temporal, bureaucratic, cognitive, and cultural constraints that have always been difficult and appear to be growing worse.

Notes

1. I. M. Destler, "National Security Advice to U.S. Presidents: Some Lessons from Thirty Years," *World Politics* 29 (January): 143–76; Leslie H. Gelb, "Why Not the State Department?" *Washington Quarterly* 1980 (Autumn): 25–40; Amy B. Zegart, *Flawed by Design: The Evolution of the CIA, JCS, and NSC* (Stanford University Press, 1999).

2. See, for example, Lincoln P. Bloomfield, "Planning Foreign Policy: Can It Be Done?" *Political Science Quarterly* 93, no. 3 (Fall 1978): 369–91; Lucian Pugliaresi and Diane T. Berliner, "Policy Analysis at the Department of State: The Policy Planning Staff," *Journal of Policy Analysis and Management* 8, no. 3 (Summer 1989): 379–94.

3. James G. March and Herbert A. Simon, *Organizations* (New York: Wiley, 1958); Herbert A. Simon, *Administrative Behavior: A Study of Decision-Making Processes in Administrative Organizations* (New York: Free Press, 1976).

4. Anthony Downs, *Inside Bureaucracy* (Upper Saddle River, N.J.: Scott Foresman, 1967); William Niskanen, "Bureaucrats and Politicians," *Journal of Law and Economics* 18 (December 1975): 617–43.

5. Graham T. Allison and Peter Szanton, *Remaking Foreign Policy* (New York: Basic Books, 1976); Diane Vaughan, *The Challenger Launch Decision: Risk Technology, Culture, and Deviance at NASA* (University of Chicago Press, 1996); James Q. Wilson, *Bureaucracy: What Government Agencies Do and Why They Do It* (New York: Basic Books, 2000); Amy B. Zegart, *Spying Blind: The CIA, the FBI, and the Origins of 9/11* (Princeton University Press, 2007).

6. Testimony of Michael Hayden, Senate Select Committee on Intelligence, "Hearing on the Confirmation of General Michael B. Hayden to become Director of the Central Intelligence Agency," 109 Cong. 2 sess., May 18, 2006.

7. Quoted in *Organizing for National Security,* study submitted to the U.S. Senate Committee on Government Operations, Subcommittee on National Policy Machinery, 87 Cong. 1 sess. (Washington: GPO, 1961), p. 8.

8. Ibid., p. 8.

9. Theodore White described the European economic situation as "a beached whale that has somehow been stranded high beyond the normal tides and which, if not rescued, will die, stink and pollute everything around it." Theodore White, *In Search of History: A Personal Adventure* (New York: Harper & Row, 1978), quoted in Wilson Miscamble, *George F. Kennan and the Making of American Foreign Policy, 1947–1950* (Princeton University Press, 1993), p. 44.

10. George Kennan, *Memoirs, 1925–1950* (New York: Pantheon, 1967), p. 325.

11. Ibid., p. 326.

12. Henry A. Kissinger, "Bureaucracy and Policy Making: The Effect of Insiders and Outsiders on the Policy Process," in Henry A. Kissinger and Bernard Brodie, *Bureaucracy, Politics, and Strategy,* Security Studies Paper 17 (University of California, Los Angeles, 1968), p. 3.

13. Ibid., pp. 2–3.

14. Ernest R. May and Philip D. Zelikow, eds., *The Kennedy Tapes: Inside the White House during the Cuban Missile Crisis* (Harvard University Press, 1997).

15. Central Intelligence Agency, *CIA World Fact Book 2008* (www.cia.gov/library/publications/the-world-factbook/ [May 1, 2008]).

16. Evan Kohlmann, "The Real Online Terrorist Threat," *Foreign Affairs* 85, no. 5 (September/October 2006); Timothy Thomas, "Al Qaeda and the Internet: The Dangers of 'Cyberplanning,'" *Parameters* (Spring 2003): 112–23; Gabriel Weimann, *Terror on the Internet: The New Arena, the New Challenges* (Washington: United States Institute of Peace Press, 2006); Lawrence Wright, "The Terror Web: Islamic Militants' Use of the Internet," *New Yorker,* August 2, 2004.

17. For Internet use statistics see www.internetworldstats.com (April 29, 2008).

18. Sara Corbett, "Can the Cell Phone Help End Global Poverty?" *New York Times Magazine,* April 13, 2008.

19. Jim Yardley, "A Hundred Cell Phones Bloom, and Chinese Take to the Streets," *New York Times,* April 25, 2005.

20. Commission on the Intelligence Capabilities of the United States Regarding Weapons of Mass Destruction (Silberman-Robb Commission), *Report to the President of the United States* (Washington: Government Printing Office, March 31, 2005), p. 5. Unclassified version at www.wmd.gov/report/index.html (January 26, 2009).

21. Testimony of Michael Hayden, May 18, 2006.

22. Zegart, *Flawed by Design.*

23. Zegart, *Spying Blind.*

24. Zegart, *Flawed by Design.*

25. Pugliaresi and Berliner, "Policy Analysis at the Department of State," p. 387.

26. Kissinger quoted in Bloomfield, "Planning Foreign Policy," p. 375.

27. Fact Sheet, U.S. Department of State Office of Public Communication, Bureau of Public Affairs, May 26, 1995 (http://dosfan.lib.uic.edu/ERC/about/fact_sheets/

950526str.html [January 26, 2009]); Hart-Rudman Commission Phase III Report, pp. 52–53 (www.fas.org/man/docs/nwc/phaseiii.pdf [December 23, 2008]).

28. Hart-Rudman Commission Phase III Report, p. 53.

29. Data set of all presidential commissions created from 1981 to 2001 in collection of author. For more, see Amy B. Zegart, "Blue Ribbons, Black Boxes: Toward a Better Understanding of Presidential Commissions," *Presidential Studies Quarterly* 34, no. 2 (June 2004): 366–93.

30. These were: the U.S. Commission on National Security in the 21st Century (Hart-Rudman Commission); the National Commission on Terrorism (Bremer Commission); the Commission to Assess the Organization of the Federal Government to Combat the Proliferation of Weapons of Mass Destruction (Deutch Commission); and the Advisory Panel to Assess Domestic Response Capabilities for Terrorism Involving Weapons of Mass Destruction (Gilmore Commission).

31. Author's analysis based on full-text Lexis/Nexis searches of ABC, CBS, NBC, CNN, Fox News, MSNBC, CNBC, and the "NewsHour with Jim Lehrer" between July 22, 2004, and December 10, 2004.

32. "Appendix B: Map of Current and Planned Fusion Centers," in Todd Masse, Siobhan O'Neil and John Rollins, *Fusion Centers: Issues and Options for Congress* (Washington: Congressional Research Service Report RL34070, July 6, 2007); Eileen R. Larence, testimony before the Senate Ad Hoc Subcommittee on State, Local, and Private Sector Preparedness and Integration, Committee on Homeland Security and Governmental Affairs, 110 Cong. 2 sess., April 17, 2008 (GAO-08-636T).

33. George Kennan, testimony before the Subcommittee on National Policy Machinery of the Committee on Government Operations, U.S. Senate, 86 Cong. 2 sess., May 26, June 17, and 27, 1960, part IV (Washington: GPO, 1960), p. 802.

34. Dean Acheson, *Present at the Creation* (New York: W. W. Norton, 1969), p. 214.

35. Robert Jervis, *Perception and Misperception in International Politics* (Princeton University Press, 1976); Daniel Kahneman, Paul Slovic, and Amos Tversky, *Judgment under Uncertainty: Heuristics and Biases* (Cambridge University Press, 1982); Daniel Kahneman and Amos Tversky, "On the Psychology of Prediction," *Psychological Review* 80 (1973): 237–51; Daniel Kahneman and Amos Tversky, "Prospect Theory: An Analysis of Decisions under Risk," *Econometrica* 47 (1979): 313–27; Amos Tversky and Daniel Kahneman, "Availability: A Heuristic for Judging Frequency and Probability," *Cognitive Psychology* 5, no. 2 (1973): 207–32.

36. Thomas Schelling, foreword to Roberta Wohlstetter, *Pearl Harbor: Warning and Decision* (Stanford University Press, 1962), p. vii.

37. Richard Betts, *Enemies of Intelligence: Knowledge and Power in American National Security* (Columbia University Press, 2007), pp. 53–65.

38. Philip E. Tetlock, *Expert Political Judgment* (Princeton University Press, 2005).

39. James Bamford, "War of Secrets: Eyes in the Sky, Ears to the Wall, and Still Wanting," *New York Times,* September 8, 2002.

40. Corbett, "Can the Cell Phone Help End Global Poverty?"

THOMAS WRIGHT

9

Learning the Right Lessons
from the 1940s

Occasionally, the question "what decade would you most like to live in?" is an interesting way of reviving a flagging dinner conversation. Among scholars and practitioners of international relations, though, the response is almost as predictable as death and taxes. I speak, of course, of the 1940s. No other decade has been cited as frequently as a model for contemporary U.S. strategy. Since September 11, 2001, everyone, from President George W. Bush to his most ardent critics, has tried to lay claim to the mantle of Presidents Roosevelt and Truman and the strategist George F. Kennan.[1] On its surface, what these men accomplished was indeed awesome. The United States was then a great power with no experience of persistent peacetime intervention in great-power politics, but it managed to design a novel grand strategy, based around international institutions, that laid the foundations for success in the postwar world. The 1940s has therefore become a holy grail to be sought and tapped to recreate a golden age of diplomacy.

Unfortunately, this narrative is based on a myth that distorts modern strategic planning. The myth is that the U.S. planning process for postwar strategy led to a successful outcome. The United States engaged in an unprecedented national effort during World War II to design a postwar strategy, but by 1946 it had irredeemably failed, as the leading U.S. statesmen of the time recognized. What was put in its place, and what ultimately worked, was the product of necessity—a response to a series of overwhelming crises—not of advance planning. That strategy evolved despite, not because of, the newly created department of policy planning. Kennan was perhaps the administration's most cogent critic; for his trouble, he was ignored and then removed from his post.

The mythology of the 1940s creates unreasonable and unrealizable expectations for grand strategy and policy planning. At worst, it may encourage grand schemes that prove counterproductive. Rather than emulating a failed process, we should seek to learn from the mistakes made, from how the Truman administration recovered from this failing, and from the sixty years of experience that we have with the order that followed. In this chapter I explain the weaknesses of U.S. strategic planning during the 1940s, and I outline six lessons that may be of use for reforming the international order today.

The Mythology of the 1940s

Before World War II, the United States traditionally remained aloof from power transitions in Europe. It occasionally sought to manipulate European politics for its own benefit on the American continent, but it avoided alliances and committed just once to intervention, during World War I, only to recoil into relative isolation after the 1919 peace talks. However, as World War II drew to a close, the United States found itself embedded in the middle of one of the great-power transition dramas in European history—the collapse of Germany, the weakening of France and Britain, and the expansion of a bruised but defiant Soviet Union.

The United States prepared for this challenge with a great national debate about postwar strategy. This debate engaged church groups, think tanks, civil society, government departments, Congress, and the public.[2] Sophisticated plans were produced and discussed. Since little could be acted upon until the war ended, this debate lasted for over four years. U.S. thinking on the postwar world, from the church group to the State Department, was dominated by a desire for something new. Americans believed that the old balance-of-power system had failed repeatedly over the previous century and a half. Only an abandonment of these practices, and a real push for comity between nations, offered hope for peace. A just international order would accommodate the legitimate security concerns of all normal states, and they could then act together against aggressor powers. Secretary of State Cordell Hull summed up the popular mood when he predicted, in 1943, "There will no longer be need for spheres of influence, for alliances, for balance of power, or any other of the special arrangements through which, in the unhappy past, the nations strove to safeguard their security in order to promote their interests."[3]

Thus the United States concerned itself with the construction of a set of universal institutions intended to remove the causes of conflict and to facilitate cooperation and the peaceful resolution of disputes against major powers.

Even former isolationists argued for a new and powerful world organization that deliberately infringed upon the sovereignty of the major powers in the name of ending war. In a series of speeches John Foster Dulles, the Republican Party's leading foreign policy spokesperson, denounced sovereignty as "inherently conducive to war," "self-destructive and a breeder of violent revolt," and "no longer consonant either with peace or with justice."[4] All this meant that the "nationalist system of independent fully sovereign states is completing its cycle of usefulness."[5]

The Roosevelt administration was bound by a national consensus that rejected balance-of-power diplomacy as a legitimate course of action for the United States. Without domestic legitimacy, the Roosevelt administration stood little chance of winning the congressional support necessary to sustain postwar internationalism. Thus Roosevelt pursued a foreign policy designed to satisfy this domestic consensus: he rejected the notion that the United States would seek to preserve a balance of power with the Soviet Union, and he championed, at least publicly, a new world organization. The apparatus of the U.S. government made the construction of this international order—the United Nations Organization and Bretton Woods—a priority. The key thing to understand is that this order was to be universal, not regional. Indeed, universalism, which meant inclusion of the Soviet Union, was at its very essence.

Placing a new world organization at the centerpiece of U.S. planning meant that the Roosevelt administration placed Soviet participation in international institutions above all other considerations. As a result, it eschewed a series of steps that would have left the United States in a better position at the end of the war. For instance the Roosevelt administration:

—Refused to collaborate bilaterally with Britain on postwar policy and negotiate collectively with the Soviet Union, despite repeated and increasingly desperate British entreaties for such an arrangement.

—Spent diplomatic capital to create the illusion that the Soviet Union would uphold basic democratic rights in Eastern Europe even though it believed that these commitments were largely worthless and that the Soviets would do as they wished.

—Refused to use material and military power to create facts on the ground that would improve the U.S.-British position vis-à-vis the Soviet Union, just as Stalin did to advance the Soviet interest and as the British wanted to do to advance theirs. The United States was more powerful than other countries during and after World War II, but it was hesitant to use its raw power in pursuit of political objectives. For instance, during the war the United States could have occupied Prague and other parts of what was to become the Eastern zone, as Churchill suggested. America could also have thrown its weight behind a British proposal to create a federation of East European states. Or it could have proposed linking the withdrawal of U.S. forces to the demarcation lines with the holding of elections in Poland. It did none of those things.

—Made almost no effort to identify U.S. global interests, to pinpoint where they might conflict with Soviet interests, and to negotiate accordingly. For instance, Roosevelt signaled disinterest toward the Dardanelles Straits and Iran, which would both become flash points in 1946. There was some thinking about "grand positioning," particularly in the Pacific, whereby the Joint Chiefs of Staff with the support of the administration sought forward basing, but not in relation to competition with the Soviet Union.

These missed opportunities might be forgivable if what was created had served its purpose, but the universality of the design meant that it fell apart once the Soviet Union acted like a rival rather than a partner. From 1944 on, the Soviet Union's actions in Eastern Europe, at international conferences, and on the Northern Tier left little doubt that it would play international politics as usual rather than participate in a transformative constitutional order. More than four years of policy planning came crashing down.

Truman stuck to Roosevelt's strategy for a while, hoping that the Soviets would come round. Repeated crises forced a change in approach. What followed is the stuff of legend—the Marshall Plan, the Truman Doctrine, and NATO—but it is absolutely vital to remember that these initiatives were not the product of deliberate thought and planning during the war; rather, they represented an immediate response to very real crises that burst on an unsuspecting public with little warning.

In fact, Kennan, head of policy planning from 1947 to 1949, was relatively uninvolved in the crafting of the Marshall Plan, and he opposed both the Truman Doctrine and NATO. Kennan had a wonderful strategic mind, but contrary to popular belief he was not very influential in the formation of U.S. strategy. He favored a classical balance-of-power strategy, with a twist. Whereas some scholars of the balance of power perceive it as a method and a goal, Kennan believed that it was a method leading to a very different end— the collapse of the Soviet Union and destruction of the political equilibrium that prevailed at the end of the war. His support for this strategy led him to favor rivalry with the Soviet Union at a very early stage and to oppose institutions that were intended to be universal in scope like the United Nations and Bretton Woods. However, it also led him to be extremely uneasy about the direction that containment took in the late 1940s, in particular the Truman Doctrine, the creation of NATO, and the thinking that lay behind NSC-68.

Indeed, if one were to compose a list of the ten people who most influenced U.S. postwar strategy in the 1940s, Kennan's name would almost certainly not be on it. It seems self-evident that Franklin D. Roosevelt, Harry Truman, Harry Hopkins, Dean Acheson, George Marshall, Paul Nitze, Arthur Vandenberg, Chip Bohlen, Averell Harriman, and James Forrestal all rank ahead of Kennan on this score. This is not to say that these men were greater strategic thinkers than Kennan; in my judgment, at that point in his career, Kennan's strategic judgment exceeded that of any other American, with the possible exception of Marshall. Rather it is to make the point that Kennan's view mattered less because it was outside the mainstream of American strategic thought.

In order to understand the 1940s it is important to distinguish between periods, particularly between the postwar planning that took place during World War II and the innovation in a time of crisis that occurred from 1947 to 1950. What succeeded in the 1940s came out of the best of traditional diplomacy—adjustment to changing international circumstances and vigorous bilateral diplomacy—and not out of advance planning. Some of the insights uncovered during the planning process proved useful to the Truman administration—the Western economic order is perhaps the best example because it was simply a more selective version of the original design—so this point should not be taken as a case against planning; rather, it should simply underscore how difficult it is to make predictions about the direction of international politics.

Five Lessons

If grand strategy in the 1940s is not the success story it is often made out to be, how should we interpret the evidence from this period in American diplomatic history? There is as much to be learned from the mistakes as from the successes. Below I offer five general lessons that may inform how today's strategists seek to reform the international order.

Be Flexible

Plans need to be flexible. Roosevelt's grand design assumed Soviet cooperation. This may have been a legitimate aspiration in 1943, but by late 1944 it was clear that it was a fiction. Similarly, the Truman strategy's greatest flaw was its doctrinal nature, which made it difficult to be prudent in resisting communism—the result was Vietnam. In a democracy, it is risky for a politician to publicly change his or her mind about a matter of great importance, but it is precisely that ability that is called for on the international stage. Consistency, while often trumpeted as a virtue, can easily lead to overextension and a lack of prudence.[6]

It is hard to offer an easy solution because the problem is cultural: to be perceived as inconsistent in a matter as grave as resisting communism or using force to prevent proliferation is not usually seen as an electoral strength by any politician. One part of the solution is for the United States to be less beholden to doctrine. Presidents should avoid universal pronunciations for fear of committing themselves without proper thought and consideration. They should also refrain from declaring a country like China or Russia to be a "partner" or a "rival." After all, a country could be one and change, or it could be both simultaneously. If Robert Kagan is right that international politics in the twenty-first century will resemble the nineteenth rather than the twentieth, it is likely that America will not face rivals as clearly "bad" as Nazi Germany and the Soviet Union.[7] Instead, the United States will worry about a clash with China over Taiwan or the future of a unified Korea while it also cooperates with Beijing to manage global capital flows and preserve stability in the global economy. The United States will compete with China for influence in Africa and Latin America while it seeks to enlist China in a global effort to tackle climate change.

With this in mind, some thought should be given to ensuring that the international order is as segmented as possible so that clashes on matters of security have little impact on cooperation in other areas. Disagreement over intervention or the responsibility to protect should not lead to a Chinese (or U.S.) walkout on economic or environmental talks. One way to advance this goal is to avoid reliance on multipurpose organizations like an expanded G-8 in favor of more focused and autonomous institutions that are established with a specific mission. These institutions should be dissolved once their mission has been accomplished.

Don't Neglect Bilateral Diplomacy

As in the 1940s, there is no institutional fix for the world, and institutions are no substitute for effective bilateral diplomacy. The Roosevelt administration worried more about the integrity of the United Nations Organization than about understanding Soviet intentions and responding accordingly. Signs of Soviet revisionism were brushed under the carpet out of fear that honesty would discredit plans to make Stalin a partner in a cooperative international order. Scarce diplomatic capital was spent on securing Soviet concessions on rules and procedures while Stalin chose to prioritize his influence in Eastern Europe.

More generally, during the course of the cold war, U.S. diplomacy was at its strongest when the president and the secretary of state sought to understand their Soviet, and Chinese, counterparts. By and large, these diplomatic missions occurred outside of international institutions. Détente, for instance, had only a small institutional component, and that was a byproduct rather than a cause of the easing in tension. None of this is to say that international institutions are not an extremely important tool. Institutions increase transparency, provide voice opportunities, facilitate collective action, and create a set of expectations and rules that countries are encouraged to live up to. However, as Robert Keohane has pointed out, all of this is dependent upon a coincidence of interest. By definition, institutions will be of more use in solidifying international friendships and maximizing the potential of alliances than in improving relations between enemies.

The modern application of this lesson is that it is less important to persuade China and Russia to sign on to a set of rules than it is to build and sustain healthy bilateral relations with each. No doubt we should welcome China and Russia to organizations like the World Trade Organization, but ultimately this means little if we forgo traditional diplomacy and understanding. During the 1990s, the West put great store in bringing Russia into the international order—economically and politically—only to see those efforts largely collapse when Vladimir Putin came to power on the eve of the millennium. Strengthening international institutions is important, and perhaps vital, but it cannot be allowed to replace traditional diplomacy, and participation in institutions cannot be the only criterion by which we measure success. The degree of trust and the length of the personal relationships between senior officials in Washington and Beijing will surely matter more at a time of grave crisis than whether China is engaged in a round of trade talks.

Strategy Needs Domestic Legitimacy

Perhaps the most important factor in U.S. strategic design during the 1940s was the need to secure and retain domestic support, without which any strategy would run the risk of falling victim to congressional opposition. Roosevelt addressed this challenge by tapping into the American people's desire for a cooperative international order, which had the effect of limiting his options. Truman used anticommunism and the Soviet threat to sell the British loan, the Marshall Plan, and NATO, all of which would have been necessary even if there had been no cold war. In each case, the Truman administration tried to secure support for the proposal strictly on its own merits, failed, and then won when it was placed in the context of the communist threat.[8] Even then, the most senior officials in government felt the need to campaign widely within the United States, as if they were running for election, to build domestic support for key foreign policy initiatives.

The need for domestic legitimacy was not confined to the 1940s. Many years later, Henry Kissinger wrote that it was the need for domestic legitimacy that ultimately doomed détente. In *Diplomacy,* he wrote:

> There was no ready constituency for Nixon's style of diplomacy . . . liberals found themselves in an uncomfortable quandary: diplomatic results of which they approved in substance, such as the relaxation of tensions with the Soviet Union and the opening to China, were emerging from principles that were anathema to the Wilsonian tradition, such as emphasis on the national interest and the balance of power. . . . To conservatives, Nixon's strategy of treating the Soviet Union as a geopolitical phenomenon was unfamiliar and uncongenial. The vast majority of them viewed the conflict with communism as being almost exclusively ideological. Convinced of America's imperviousness to geopolitical challenges, they treated issues at the front lines of containment as being of marginal concern and as too close for comfort to the traditional struggles of the European powers, which, on the whole they held in low esteem.[9]

Today the international order is suffering a crisis of confidence, both in the United States and abroad. Long before the international financial crisis exposed the shortcomings of the international financial architecture, this was evident in the collapse of congressional support for free trade, the ease with which President Bush disengaged from multilateral organizations in his first term, popular worldwide protests against the G-8, the French, Dutch, and Irish rejection of various EU treaties, the collapse in support for the International Monetary Fund (IMF) in Asia, and the stresses and strains in the international nonproliferation regime. The economic historian Harold James has observed that "the currently prevalent way of thinking about globalization simply as a system of interconnections, of processes and networks that span national and cultural boundaries is bound to produce a backlash, primarily because it is widely assumed that this is simply a euphemism for some sort of imperial rule."[10] In other words, if the public believes that a strategic plan exists solely for the purpose of keeping the wheels of the machine well oiled, they will be less likely to support it than if they believed it represented a strategic or moral imperative.

What is missing is glue to hold the project together—whether it be common values or a shared threat. The United States and its allies will have to find some normative basis for reform of the international order if they are to secure sufficient domestic support to allow it to take place. Statesmen may have to take a leaf out of Acheson and Truman's playbook and actively campaign throughout their countries, for a prolonged period of time, to convince their fellow citizens of the benefits of major international commitments.

Problem Solving Matters More than the Legitimacy Deficit

While it is true that the world looks very different in 2009 than it did in 1945, it would be a mistake to begin reform efforts with changes in the governance structure of international institutions. The aim is laudable, but "Who rules?" is one of the perennially difficult of all the questions in world politics, and it is frequently perceived as zero-sum. An effort to reform the UN Security Council first will get bogged down in regional rivalries as China vetoes Japan, Argentina blocks Brazil, and so on. Similarly, reweighting the voting at the IMF will prove immensely controversial in Europe, as would removing countries from the G-8. Such initiatives will simply suck up all of the oxygen and leave no room for other reforms that are arguably much more important.

The 1940s show that major foreign policy initiatives stood a greater chance of success when they were a response to major and immediate problems—such as the collapse of the European economy, Soviet intervention on the Northern Tier, the need for Franco-German cooperation to facilitate German rearmament—than when they anticipated those problems. Therefore the United States should prioritize institutional reform that is specifically targeted to modern problems like climate change, the management of global capital flows, nuclear proliferation, and so on. Of these, the greatest scope for institutional innovation lies in the area of climate change and the global economy. The first is a concern that simply was not imagined in the 1940s, while the second has changed so fundamentally as to raise real questions about the relevance of the organizations created at the end of World War II. Over time, legitimacy concerns can be addressed as new institutions are created.

Manage Expectations for Policy Planning, Specifically and Generally

The 1940s demonstrate that it is impossible to implement a strategy as sophisticated, rich, and controversial as Kennan's from the perch of policy planning. As noted earlier, Kennan lobbied hard for a balance-of-power approach to the Soviet Union, opposing both universal institutions and the Truman Doctrine in turn. To draw a parallel, try to imagine Henry Kissinger in the same position serving a secretary of state and a president who did not share his vision. The only way in which an approach like Kennan's or Kissinger's can stand any chance of success is if its strongest advocates occupy the highest possible positions in the foreign policymaking process, and even then it would require a nontrivial dollop of bureaucratic skill. Grand strategic change must reflect the passions and interests of the president. Otherwise, it must articulate an overwhelming consensus among the foreign policy decisionmakers within the government. It has never succeeded as a minority viewpoint from outside the Oval Office.

More generally, the ability of the United States to shape international institutions will be more limited than it was in the 1940s. The Bretton Woods order was largely the creation of the world's two major economic powers, which happened to be the United States and Great Britain, with negotiations tilted heavily in favor of the former. Today, America's economic peers are not necessarily her political allies and will not feel the need to defer to Washington's will without proper and meaningful consultation. Therefore, there can be no 100-day plan announced on day one because the United States cannot unilaterally remake multilateralism. Instead, the next president should lead an international conversation about how to reform the architecture of international cooperation.

Conclusion

A number of the other chapters in this book point out that it's not the plans but the planning that really matters. Bruce Jentleson sums this up when he favorably quotes Eisenhower's remark, "The plans are nothing but the planning is everything." Of course, it always makes sense to devote systematic thought to key strategic challenges, but it is also worth pointing out some limitations.

The distinction between planning and plans is more artificial in diplomacy than it is in the military, for two reasons. First, military plans are often not implemented until the president makes a conscious decision to launch military action. However, diplomatic plans are frequently implemented on a rolling basis from a very early stage in the planning process—diplomats take a certain tack in negotiations and other avenues are closed off. During World War II, this meant the pursuit of a universal order and the rejection of other options. Therefore, in diplomacy, the plans and the planning are linked to a far greater degree than is true in military planning. Second, the failure of a military plan is frequently more observable than the failure of a diplomatic plan. In war, an invasion may be repelled, assets may be lost, and ground may be conceded, but in diplomacy failure can come a drop at a time but be no less lethal as a result.

In this chapter I have argued that many of the strategic mistakes in the 1940s stem from a series of false assumptions that constrained and distorted the strategic planning process. Planning is indispensable, but only if it is not flawed by design. Therefore the challenge that policymakers face is to get the process right—to ensure that strategic thinkers are encouraged to be practical and flexible enough to challenge prevailing assumptions and adjust to changing circumstances, not to allow grand plans to be a substitute for traditional bilateral diplomacy, to build domestic support for foreign policy, to address real problems and crises rather than seek utopia, and to have modest expectations.

The shortcomings in U.S. postwar planning were understood decades ago. In the 1950s and 1960s scholars such as Kennan, Kissinger, and Hans Morgenthau argued that during World War II, and immediately following its conclusion, American postwar planning was beset by idealism and naïveté, that the United States did not pay enough attention to material power between 1942 and 1947, and that its later strategy of containment went too far in its universalism. This interpretation, at least the part leading up to 1947, was brutally attacked and began to disappear when the traditionalist-revisionist-postrevisionist cold war debate was joined in the 1970s. In the 1990s, after the collapse of the Soviet Union, the transformation was completed. Structural realists began to use American strategy as the poster child for state behavior while liberal scholars praised U.S. farsightedness, particularly with respect to its attitude toward institutions, which played a crucial role in containment's eventual success.

The result is that Kennan, Morgenthau, and Kissinger's critique has been forgotten, even though it has been strengthened by the release of evidence from the Soviet archives, which shows Stalin taking advantage of American naïveté. That the U.S. record is mixed should not be surprising; the times were trying, by any standard, and the country was new to playing such a pivotal global role. There is as much to be learned from the failures as from the successes, which means that a clear-headed assessment of the moment of creation, as Dean Acheson put it, is long overdue.

Notes

1. For example, see G. John Ikenberry, *After Victory: Institutions, Strategic Restraint, and the Rebuilding of Order after Major War* (Princeton University Press, 2001); G. John Ikenberry, *America Unrivaled: The Future of the Balance of Power* (Cornell University Press, 2002). Also see Peter Beinart, *The Good Fight; Why Liberals and*

Only Liberals Can Win the War on Terror and Make America Great Again (New York: HarperCollins, 2006). For an account of how President Bush and his critics tried to embrace Truman, see James Goldgeier and Derek Chollet, "The Truman Standard" *American Interest* 1, no. 4 (Summer 2006): 107–11.

2. See Harley Notter, *Postwar Foreign Policy Preparation, 1939–1945* (Washington: Department of State, 1950); Robert A. Divine, *Second Chance; The Triumph of Internationalism in America during World War II* (New York: Atheneum, 1967); Patrick Hearden, *Architects of Globalism: Building a New World Order during World War II* (University of Arkansas Press, 2002).

3. Cordell Hull, address before Congress regarding the Moscow Conference, November 18, 1943, in *U.S. Department of State Bulletin* IX, no. 230 (November 20, 1943): 343.

4. John Foster Dulles, "A North American Contribution to World Order," speech to the 3rd Conference on Canadian-American Affairs, June 20, 1939 (John Foster Dulles Papers [JFDP], Seely Mudd Library, Princeton University, Box 289); Dulles, "America's Role in World Affairs," Address to the National Council of Young Men's Christian Associations of Detroit, October 28, 1939 (JFDP, Box 289); Dulles, address at the Second Presbyterian Church, Philadelphia, Penn., March 12, 1941 (JFDP, Box 290).

5. Dulles, "America's Role in World Affairs."

6. What is perhaps more surprising than the intransigence of politicians is the intransigence of scholars. The Bush years saw a great debate on grand strategy, but it is hard to think of any grand strategist who radically changed his or her position as the world changed. "The world has changed profoundly, and this proves that I was right all along" sums up the mood.

7. Robert Kagan, *The Return of History and the End of Dreams* (New York: Knopf, 2008),

8. The best account of this dynamic is by Richard Freeland, *The Truman Doctrine and the Origins of McCarthyism: Foreign Policy, Domestic Politics, and Internal Security 1946–1948* (New York: Alfred A. Knopf, 1972).

9. Henry A. Kissinger, *Diplomacy* (New York: Simon and Schuster, 1994), p. 743.

10. Harold James, "Globalization, Empires, and Natural Law," *International Affairs* 84, no. 3 (2008): 423.

ANDREW P. N. ERDMANN

10

Foreign Policy Planning through a Private Sector Lens

At the start of the twenty-first century, the United States confronts profound foreign policy challenges. Consider the unraveling of the global financial system, the rise of the so-called BRIC countries (Brazil, Russia, India, and China) and the erosion of the United States' relative power in the world, climate change and energy policy, the proliferation of technologies of potential mass destruction, and the cascading implications of state weakness and failure. Appreciating the complex interplay of long-term trends is a prerequisite for developing policies to manage, if not solve, such challenges. The U.S. government, however, lacks a standing strategic planning process to inform the decisions of today with such a long-term perspective.[1]

This chapter attempts to glean potential insights for the planning of foreign policy from the private sector's experience with strategic planning. America's business is famously business. The boundary between private and public sector service in the United States is more permeable than that in other advanced industrial and postindustrial states. Yet discussions of foreign policy planning usually overlook private sector experience. Instead, they invoke other public sector experience—looking to past precedent or to the military's approach to planning.[2] The professional backgrounds of foreign policy planners reflect this reality. In the first sixty years of the secretary of state's policy planning staff, only one of its twenty-four directors arrived with significant private sector experience. Diplomats, lawyers, academics, and think tank policy analysts have been the norm.[3]

To be sure, we should be cautious about prescribing private sector remedies for public sector ailments. Differences between the two spheres are significant, in terms of clarity of authority, ability to make staffing decisions, conceptions of "efficiency," and above all their respective "bottom lines."[4] Moreover, when private sector "best practices" are misapplied in the public sector, the results can make you feel as though you stumbled into a Dilbert cartoon. Consumers and producers alike of poorly conceived "metrics" and stoplight charts, or half-hearted vision statements and annual "objectives," can testify to this uncomfortable feeling of caricature.

This chapter nonetheless seeks to demonstrate the potential for mutually beneficial exchange across the private-public sector border. Strategic planning is a particularly attractive topic with which to experiment in such trade. First, both sectors face similar challenges in this area. Although their "bottom lines" differ, they share the fundamental dilemma of finding how (in the apt words of James Steinberg) to "bring the future into the present" to inform major decisions.[5] Both must take into account potential responses by competitors and reactions of numerous external stakeholders—the press, civic groups and nongovernmental organizations, formal and informal regulators, and others.[6] Both confront the enduring dilemma of how the urgent drives the important off a decisionmaker's agenda. And both aim ultimately to translate ideas into decisions that move complex organizations to action. Second, the private sector's experience with strategic planning is diverse and deep. Different approaches have been tested, new ones developed. Business executives have written memoirs, and have been surveyed, interviewed, and analyzed, to create a library on business strategy. In sum, there is much material to trade.

Exploring selected themes in private sector thought regarding strategic planning—supported by illustrative examples drawn from corporate practice—provides a different lens through which to view the challenge of foreign policy planning.[7] Doing so may help foreign policy specialists see familiar things in new ways. The goal is to illuminate how strategic planning processes have evolved in the private sector and why they should be considered part of the broader challenge of "strategic management" that encompasses planning as well as execution. The private sector's conception of strategists' role is also evolving. Although the strategic planning process matters, business history reminds us that there is only so much that process can accomplish over the long haul. More often than not, the market eventually wins. Developing, implementing, and then reinventing successful strategies is a Herculean task that few achieve.

Buyer Beware: Frustrations with "Traditional" Strategic Planning

At first blush, the answer to the foreign policy planning challenge might appear simple: import "traditional" private sector strategic planning approaches directly into the government. This could involve empowering strategic planning groups to analyze the future, define objectives, review different units' proposed plans, generate robust policy options, and formulate integrated plans that synchronize policy with budgeting and resource allocation.

These are the activities people usually think of when they hear "strategic planning." This traditional model of strategic planning was raised by General Electric to an art form in corporate America during the 1960s and 1970s.[8] With decades of practice and experience generating plans and annual reviews in multiple industries, the vice presidents and directors of strategy in the private sector must be doing something right. Strategic planning may be the most-used private sector management tool in the world. Its very popularity suggests satisfaction and performance.[9]

When one peels the onion, however, a different image appears. To be sure, variations on the "traditional" model of planning can work—as demonstrated by the successes at Emerson Electric under CEO Chuck Knight and AlliedSignal and then Honeywell under CEO Larry Bossidy.[10] But these are the exceptions rather than the rule. Anecdotes abound in the private sector about stale and cumbersome annual planning processes that produce little beyond voluminous briefing binders. "Our planning process is like some primitive tribal ritual," one executive quipped. "There is a lot of noise, dancing, waving of feathers, beating of drums, and no one is sure exactly why we do it, but still there is an almost mystical hope that something good will eventually come of it, and it never does."[11] Reflecting on his company's strategic planning process, another manager concluded: "It's like the old Communist system: We pretend to make strategy and they pretend to follow it."[12] When Jack Welch took over as CEO of General Electric (GE) in 1981, some staffers were grading planning books by the "pizzazz on each cover. It was nuts."[13]

Recent surveys of executives go beyond anecdotes to reveal more systematically the widespread dissatisfaction with most annual strategic planning processes. A Marakon Associates and the Economist Intelligence Unit survey revealed that only 11 percent were "highly satisfied" with their strategic planning process.[14] Results from a 2006 *McKinsey Quarterly* survey of global executives are slightly better, but still not encouraging. Only 45 percent replied that they were satisfied with their strategic planning process.[15]

Why the "frustration, if not outright antipathy" felt by most executives? First, process. In many corporations, individual business units conduct strategic planning on an established annual cycle, and the plans are then reviewed, business unit by business unit. However, 100 percent of executives report making strategic decisions year round, without regard to any planning calendar. Moreover, 70 percent make their decisions on an issue-by-issue basis, across business unit boundaries. The planning process often does not fit the normal decisionmaking rhythm. As witnessed during the Wall Street turmoil in 2008, opportunities and threats can materialize with alarming speed; the odds are against such developments being serendipitously synchronized with an established planning calendar.[16] While a majority of those whose companies have a formal strategic planning process feel it contributes significantly to developing corporate strategy, less than one quarter report their companies make important strategic decisions within the formal strategic planning process.[17]

Second, content. Formal strategic planning processes too often become (as suggested earlier) annual rituals with little impact. Only a slight majority of executives report that their strategic planning processes focus on the "most important strategic issues facing the company, not tactical issues." Furthermore, only 43 percent believe that the strategic planning process prioritizes substantive discussion over process, and less than 30 percent believe it fosters creativity.[18] Most business unit strategies fail to provide more than one option to executives or consider potential competitor responses, even though most executives believe these tasks are important. Only a slight majority of business units regularly assess the top trends shaping their business environment in the next three to five years.[19] Finally, the traditional model of strategic planning's foundational premises—that is, that strategy is something that can be planned well in advance and can be detached from operations—is increasingly dubious.[20] Annual reviews can devolve into truncated, scripted discussions. Too often, strategy reviews "amount to little more than business tourism."[21] "Strategic planning at most companies doesn't really matter anymore," strategy consultant Michael Mankins bluntly concludes.[22]

New Approaches to Strategic Planning

In the face of such widespread frustration with strategic planning, one could easily swing to the other extreme—namely, that the private sector offers no useful insights to the public sector.

But the onion needs to be peeled again. Overall impressions mask some successful innovations. Executives recognize the need to find some way to bring the future into the present. What we have seen in the past few decades are efforts to redefine our expectations for strategic planning, to develop new approaches to focus leadership attention on macro, long-term challenges, and to discover new formal and informal mechanisms to bring insights from strategic planning to bear on major decisions wherever they are made—in the boardroom, in the hallway, or on the eighteenth green.

As a first step, we should recognize that no single unified model for strategic planning exists. As McGill University management scholar Henry Mintzberg argues, we expand our understanding of what strategy is and can be by imaging a spectrum spanning from "deliberate" strategies to "emergent" ones. "Deliberate strategy" fits with the common dictionary definition and everyday usage to mean a "plan" that is consciously formulated to achieve certain defined objectives. This conception views strategy as translating a strategist's intent into specific, codified plans to guide an organization's conduct. More often than not, this is what people reflexively imagine when they hear the word "strategy." Marking the other end of the spectrum, though, are "emergent strategies." Instead of looking to intended plans, Herbert Simon defined strategy as "the series of . . . decisions which determines behavior over some stretch of time." From this perspective, organizations can possess strategies whether or not they ever formally develop a plan; their strategies "emerge" as patterns from their actions.[23]

Although we often think of strategies as the product of intent and deliberation, many successful strategies just emerge. Interviews with founders of successful new ventures, for instance, reveal that two-thirds had no business plan or only a "rudimentary" one before launching their business. They succeeded nonetheless through learning and adaptation.[24] Major industry leaders have also followed emergent paths to successful strategies. Looking back on the spectacular turnaround by British Petroleum, former CEO Lord Browne described the process as "a series of steps, each building on the last, but without a predetermined plan."[25] There is also a cautionary note here: we tend to look for deliberate strategies, even where none exist. In the 1970s a famous Boston Consulting Group analysis of the English motorcycle industry's decline made this mistake by suggesting that Honda's market entry strategy for the United States reflected a careful, deliberate strategy. In fact, interviews with the leaders of the Honda effort subsequently revealed a fitful process of trial-and-error and adaptation.[26]

Debating the merits of different strategic approaches is a veritable cottage industry in the business literature. These debates should not obscure Mintzberg's foundational insight: "Strategy formulation walks on two feet, one deliberate, the other emergent. . . . The relative emphasis may shift from time to time but not the requirement to attend to both sides of this phenomenon."[27]

The implications of this insight are profound. "This notion that both emergence and deliberation are necessary changes our view of the strategist's task," concludes Harvard Business School's Jan Rivkin. "The challenge is not to design a great strategy, but to design a search process that will uncover a great strategy."[28] Similarly, McKinsey consultants Eric Beinhocker and Sarah Kaplan argue that "a key starting point is the acceptance of the counterintuitive notion that the strategic-planning process should not be designed to *make strategy.*"[29] To reiterate, executives make decisions with strategic impact continually, usually outside any regular planning process. So what should the strategic planning process be about? For starters, it should help executives identify major trends affecting their companies, devise creative options, and make informed decisions. But formal strategic planning's "real value," Kaplan and Beinhocker highlight, is as "a learning tool to create 'prepared minds' within their organizations (to paraphrase Louis Pasteur)."[30]

Royal Dutch/Shell Group's scenario planning in the 1970s and 1980s is probably the most widely known example of the private sector's strategic planning innovations. Royal Dutch/Shell Group's scenario approach involves developing alternative "histories of the future" that blend rigorous, fact-based analysis with creative panache, to help decisionmakers confront potential uncertainties, risks, and opportunities and formulate their strategies accordingly. Scenarios are not about prediction, but mental preparation. As Pierre Wack, the leader of Shell's scenario team during its "golden age" in the 1970s, concluded, scenarios are "a creative experience that generates a heartfelt 'Aha!' from your management and leads to strategic insights beyond the mind's previous reach." Such achievement is rare indeed. The Royal Dutch/Shell Group scenario team scored its first distinctive success in 1972 and 1973 when its scenarios imagined a severe global energy crisis and thereby prepared the corporate leadership to adapt more rapidly than competitors. This and other successes, including anticipation of the implosion of the Soviet Union, are widely credited with helping Royal Dutch/Shell Group eclipse many of its rivals. No matter how ingenious the scenarios themselves, however, the scenario team would have achieved little if not for an executive team that supported them, listened to them, and took them seriously.[31]

General Electric's transformation of its strategic planning approach is also instructive. Shortly after taking over as CEO, Jack Welch decided to dismantle the annual corporate strategic planning process that had been constructed over the previous two decades. "Take a look around you," he told the assembled corporate strategic planners when he first met them in 1981, "because you won't be seeing each other anymore."[32] Welch did not scrap formal planning entirely, but pushed responsibility from the corporate planners to the business unit leaders and then established an intense annual strategic planning dialogue with his top executive team. Out went the briefing binders with their reams of data prepared by strategic planning staff; in came tightly written five-page memorandums for each business summarizing its "current market dynamics, the competitor's key recent activities, the GE business response, the greatest competitive threat over the next three years, and the GE business's planned response." He reviewed personally the plans for every GE business, often in grueling ten- to twelve-hour sessions to ensure strategic alignment throughout the organization. But businesses did not have to produce a plan formulaically every year, unless there was reason for a review. Later, in the 1990s, Welch pushed GE to unleash its creativity by establishing "stretch" performance targets with—he later admitted—"no real idea of how to get there." These goals compelled the search for innovative solutions. Finally, Welch recognized that GE management had to focus on understanding and responding to a few long-term trends shaping the business environment; these did not fit within the regular business unit reviews. Therefore, he drove through the annual Operating Managers Meeting of the top 500 GE executives a series of multiyear, cross-cutting strategic initiatives, including Six Sigma quality control, "e-business," globalization, and services.[33]

Johnson & Johnson in the 1990s provides another example of how an established firm experimented with its planning process to inject greater innovation and broader, longer-term perspective. The near collapse of IBM in the early 1990s cast a long shadow over corporate America: if "Big Blue" could fail, any company could, regardless of pedigree. The Johnson & Johnson leadership concluded that it needed a new approach to identify potential long-term threats and opportunities, and help align decisionmaking in a decentralized corporation of 170 operating companies spread around the world. The semistructured "FrameworkS" process was born. (Symbolically, the concluding capital "S" underscored the embrace of multiple perspectives.) The corporate nine-person Executive Committee consciously shifted its attention from individual business units to broader cross-cutting issues such as the "new American consumer," regional growth in Asia, and innovation. The Executive Committee appointed a team drawn from throughout the organization, which then divided into separate task forces to research topics related to the overarching theme for up to six months. During multiday meetings, the Executive Committee discussed the results with the FrameworkS working team. As then CEO Ralph Larson described the process: "We are not seeking concrete answers at these sessions, although some do emerge. The aim is to interact in a spirit of openness. Assumptions are cast aside. Everything is challenged. We are literally starting from scratch, and the exercise can be invigorating, startling, painful—and extraordinarily rewarding." The sessions generated new initiatives and businesses; equally important, the process helped forge "a productive collaboration among our Executive Committee and operating leadership worldwide."[34]

Google is famously an innovative company, wildly successful in its first decade, and an exemplar of a much less structured approach to planning. Google's founders, Sergey Brin and Larry Page, appreciate the role luck played in their original success and take nothing for granted: Google must constantly innovate to survive. Therefore they are self-consciously trying to build an organization that foments innovation to drive the rapid evolution needed to keep pace with technology, systems, customers, and competitors. The bedrock of its approach to planning is small, ad hoc teams and innovation "from below." The leadership establishes the tone. To kick off Google's first formal planning process, CEO Eric Schmidt posed broad questions such as "How could the company get its services on hundreds of millions of mobile phones?" and then established teams to tackle them. Significantly, the teams decided that the original questions were not very interesting and struck off in their own direction. Schmidt welcomed this dynamism: "The group interactions were terrific" and "They developed some really intriguing ideas." Furthermore, Schmidt and his staff devote up to six hours each week during "product strategy meetings" in order to speak with team members throughout the company. These keep Schmidt and his team close to the grassroots innovators. Perhaps most important, company policy allows each employee to devote 20 percent of his or her time to independent projects. Teams self-organize to pursue sometimes outlandish innovations. Many fail, but independent projects also build enthusiasm, help attract talent, and importantly, sometimes succeed. At times, the majority of Google's new products launched have originated in a "20 percent project."[35]

In practice, therefore, private sector planning ranges from the more formal and "deliberate" to the decentralized and explicitly "emergent." Besides Shell, GE, Johnson & Johnson, and Google, many other companies have rethought their annual planning processes. Companies as diverse as Microsoft, Cadbury Schweppes, Textron, and Cardinal Health, for instance, have embraced the idea of continuous strategic dialogue focused on a select few cross-cutting issues.[36] Taken together, we see efforts to supplement—and even replace—top management's focus on formulaic annual financial planning and budgeting with more fluid, in-depth investigations of selected strategic themes. Influential business theorist Richard Rumelt, for instance, now advocates the creation of a "nonannual, opportunity-driven process for strategy work" separate from annual resource planning.[37] Corporate leaders increasingly appreciate that how such investigations are conducted can be as important as their final content. Carefully prepared dialogue about emerging trends and their implications among executives is a much more powerful way to "prepare minds" than yet another series of deadening PowerPoint slides prepared by and for strategy staffs.[38]

From Strategic Planning to Strategic Management

Robert Bowie, the third director of the State Department's policy planning staff, often said that the purpose of a planner "is not merely to produce literature, but to produce results."[39] Every would-be strategist should remember this common-sense wisdom. Identifying and analyzing strategic trends and then generating creative policy options are necessary, but hardly sufficient.

Implementation matters, often most of all. Over the past two decades, multiple studies have revealed that "60% to 80% of companies fall short of the success predicted from their new strategies."[40] Without grounding in the realities of execution, any strategy risks becoming an academic exercise.[41]

Instead of framing the challenge as improving "strategic planning," therefore, it is more productive to view it as one of improving "strategic management." When the term "strategic management" first came into vogue in the late 1970s, McKinsey & Company consultants defined its core features in ways that still remain useful. Strategic management is "the melding of strategic planning and everyday management into a single, seamless process. . . . No longer is planning a yearly, or even quarterly, activity. Instead, it is woven into the fabric of operational decision making." Strategic management involves not just a strategic framework, strategic planning capabilities, and a process to make resource trade-offs among alternatives, but also a "performance review system that focuses the attention of top managers on key problems and opportunity areas" and a "motivational system and management values that reward and promote the exercise of strategic thinking."[42]

Effective strategic management typically involves five core steps: develop strategy; translate strategy into specific objectives, metrics and targets, and initiatives; plan operations, including budgeting; monitor regularly and review strategy; and last, test and adapt the strategy. Devising the right "scorecards" and "dashboards" is critical to help leaders focus on the most important "levers" to pull. Ideally, these processes reinforce and are reinforced by personnel policies, information technology, and other supporting systems. Ultimately, the goal is to create the mind-sets, behaviors, and processes that infuse strategy development with rigor and creativity, as well as clear and consistent accountability in its execution. When done right, a virtuous cycle begins.[43]

The GE Operating System developed under Jack Welch's leadership relied on a strategy and operations review process that was emotionally and intellectually exhausting. But his approach to strategic management did not end there. Welch concluded early on that GE's success ultimately hinged on attracting, developing, and retaining top talent. "The GE leader sees this company for what it truly is," Welch said, "the largest petri dish for business innovation in the world." He focused accordingly on putting in place the institutions, incentives, and processes to ensure GE executives could both conceive and execute ambitious business plans. Welch drove a leadership development process that ruthlessly weeded out low performers and richly rewarded stars who exemplified GE's values and delivered results. Welch personally tracked the top 500 executives in GE, every one of whom he had appointed. He transformed the compensation system by expanding the stock options program and increasing bonuses tied to performance on strategic initiatives or other priorities. Under his leadership, GE's Crotonville leadership center changed from a backwater into an engine of cultural change. Walking the walk, Welch traveled to Crotonville twice a month to teach, personally communicate his vision and priorities, and meet with managers from around the world.[44] Welch's investments in leadership development continue to pay dividends: GE has more alumni who are CEOs for major U.S. corporations than any other company.[45]

The strategic management system implemented by CEO Sir Terry Leahy has proven critical to Tesco PLC's dramatic turnaround from an also-ran British supermarket chain in the early 1990s to an international juggernaut of retail alongside America's Wal-Mart and France's Carrefour today. While deeply skeptical of what he calls "management gobbledygook," Leahy picked up a copy of Professor Robert Kaplan's books on the "balanced-scorecard" management system and eventually became one of Kaplan's most devoted disciples. The balanced-scorecard approach provides a more complete picture of an organization's performance and health by tracking not only traditional financial metrics, but also intangibles such as customer satisfaction, operational performance, employee quality, training, and morale, and more recently, corporate social responsibility. Tesco adopted the system in the late 1990s and developed an integrated set of processes to monitor as well as motivate performance throughout its 400,000-plus workforce. Tesco's uses a distinctive "Steering Wheel" graphic to represent its scorecard. Currently it has just twenty "spokes"—each one representing a key metric that is monitored throughout the organization, down to the local market. Management reviews the Steering Wheel quarterly and also regularly reassesses the spokes to ensure that they reflect the major drivers of Tesco's overall strategy. Whereas many efforts to use a balanced scorecard fail, Tesco has brought the approach to life by making it real to everyone in the organization. Metrics are not reported and forgotten, they are linked directly to promotions and compensation, integrated in training materials, and appear throughout corporate reports. Tesco has also invested in sophisticated systems to track some metrics in real time. For example, one metric for customer satisfaction is "I don't queue"—that is, the customer does not have to wait in line long to check out. Some Tesco stores have plasma TV screens above each checkout register that monitor in real time the average wait time throughout the day; as soon as the indicators flag, a manager can shift staff to open extra lines and reduce wait time. In this way, strategic priorities shape action down to the store level every day to ensure consistent execution.[46]

General Electric, Tesco, and other companies such as Emerson Electric prove that process does matter. Strategic planning can only translate into success if it is woven into a complex web of mutually reinforcing activities—such as compensation and promotion—as part of a broader strategic management process. These companies also highlight how difficult weaving such a tapestry can be. Many go through the motions of adopting the latest management fad, but ignore the basics.[47] Yet organizations can assimilate new ways of doing business.[48] It just takes years of dedicated effort.

So Who Is the Strategist Now?

But who should drive this process? Who should be the strategist in an organization? Three basic lessons emerge from recent business practice and thought.

First, leadership of the strategic management process cannot be outsourced. The CEO must own the strategy. This goes beyond providing strategic direction or making difficult trade-off decisions. Leaders communicate what they value and expect through their actions and thereby help define their organization's priorities and shape its culture. Employees notice—consciously and subconsciously—any gap between what leaders say and what they do. A CEO and his or her leadership team must retain a near monomaniacal focus and prioritization to ensure that this gap remains small; if it does not, doubts emerge (in the leader and among his or her team and the rank and file), enthusiasm and focus flag, and "old ways" reassert themselves.[49]

This is not a simplistic call for "charismatic" or visionary leadership. Successful leaders master the internal processes, incentives, and other "levers" that move complex organizations to action. This holds true whether a company pursues primarily a deliberate strategy or an emergent one. Chuck Knight estimates that he devoted 60 percent of his time to planning processes—weaving strategic, operational, and personnel plans into a seam-less whole—during his twenty-seven years as CEO of Emerson. Larry Bossidy committed himself to a similarly intensive and lengthy strategic plan and operating plan reviews. He underscored how seriously he viewed the process by following up every review with personal letters to business unit heads in which he reiterated priorities and expectations for the next review. Jack Welch spent approximately 70 percent of his time on people issues, learning firsthand the strengths and weaknesses of GE's global leadership team, whose activities ranged from the production of jet engines to medical imaging devices to light bulbs to nuclear power plant equipment. Ralph Larson and the Johnson & Johnson leadership team embraced the FrameworkS process and then com-mitted the time to make it work. Every day Google's leaders show their sup-port for innovation by how they commit their time and resources.

Second, strategy's content cannot be outsourced either. Strategic plans can-not be left to the planners alone; those who will implement strategy should be involved in its development. They bring practical awareness of emergent issues and opportunities, an on-the-ground perspective of the operating environ-ment, and keen understanding of potential implementation challenges. Equally important, operators and line executives need to be involved to build genuine ownership. Operators have their own strategic perspectives and the power to create "facts on the ground" through countless operational deci-sions that shape a strategy's success. Without their understanding and sup-port, a strategy will stall. Dialogue between the leadership and the implementers is critical to help each calibrate expectations, synchronize pri-orities, and establish shared expectations and commitment. This is a theme running through approaches from companies as diverse as Emerson Electric, Johnson & Johnson, GE, and Google. In the end, though, the leadership must make the tough trade-off decisions and make them stick.[50]

Is there then any the role left for all those who formally have "strategy" in their title? If everyman is a strategist of sorts, is there a need for dedicated strategy groups? The idea that specialized planning staffs should formulate strategy for a CEO to approve and line managers to implement is long dead. In its place, new, more restrained, but realistic roles for in-house strategists are emerging.

Thus, third, "planners should make their contributions *around* the strat-egy-making process rather than *inside* it."[51] The planning staff can serve as the "conveners of the conversations," designing and running a strategy develop-ment process that helps inform and align executives throughout an organi-zation on priorities and direction. They can be the intellectual provocateurs when needed. They can undertake the necessary analyses to ensure that strategy discussions are fact-based dialogues. They can help identify important "over-the-horizon" topics that merit senior executive attention through formal reviews or more informal dialogues such as Johnson & Johnson's FrameworkS series. They also can help develop metrics, communicate the strategic plan, and monitor its implementation. Finally, strategists can serve as internal consultants, assisting business units with their strategy development or undertaking special projects for the leadership. C-level executives (that is, those whose titles begin with "chief") believe the internal consulting role should be a top priority for their strategic planners.[52]

We may even be entering a new era for strategists. Some have labeled strategic management an "emerging profession."[53] A new C-level executive role is becoming increasingly popular in corporate America: the chief strategy officer (CSO). Companies as diverse as Cisco and Campbell's Soup now have one. CSOs serve as their CEO's deputy for strategy. J. F. Van Kerckhove, vice president of corporate strategy at eBay, describes the role as "helping to coordinate and inject knowledge in the more formal strategy process, as well as fostering an environment for more spontaneous strategy creation."[54] This involves helping the CEO and the leadership team achieve alignment on a strategy, and then clarifying its implications for the rest of the organization. To be effective, a CSO should be "deeply trusted by the CEO," comfortable with ambiguity, objective and able to speak truth to power, a master of persuasion to rally other executives, and last, a "doer, not just a thinker." The final point is significant: most CSOs come with significant operational experience and do not consider themselves career strategists. Instead, they often view a CSO role as a stepping-stone to running a business.[55]

The Never-Ending Race of Strategy

If the long and diverse private sector experience is any guide, it teaches humility to any strategist. Few companies survive and thrive over the long haul—despite numerous best sellers that promise easy ten-step programs to enduring success.

The numbers are humbling. For example, in 1987 *Forbes* magazine republished its original 1917 listing of the 100 largest companies in America and asked what had happened to them. In seventy years, sixty-one firms had disappeared entirely through bankruptcy or mergers. Twenty-one others survived but slipped out of the top 100. Only eighteen endured in the top 100 for seventy years—including Procter and Gamble, Citibank, and Exxon. One might assume that these great companies that survived the Great Depression, World War II, the cold war, and the dramatic transformations in the U.S. economy would also be top performers. But only two—General Electric and Kodak—performed above the market average during those seventy years. Soon thereafter, Kodak's performance slipped, leaving General Electric as the sole survivor from the original Forbes 100 that consistently outperformed the market. Another study showed that only about 1 percent of companies achieve repeat excellence—that is, return to superior performance after a setback. A 1 percent long-term survival and success rate should give any strategist pause.[56]

Whether in the private sector or in foreign policy, the strategist confronts an endless cycle of competition, called a "Red Queen race" after the Red Queen in Lewis Carroll's *Through the Looking Glass.* "There is no such thing as winning a Red Queen race," business strategist Eric Beinhocker concludes. "The best you can ever do is run faster than the competition."[57] The strategist's job is not just extraordinarily difficult, but also never done.

This harsh reality may help explain another common feature among the companies surveyed here: none is complacent. Whether the Johnson & Johnson leadership stunned by the fall of IBM or the Google leadership self-conscious of its own sudden rise, their approaches have been animated by instinctive appreciation that there is little margin for error. They share in deed if not in word former Intel CEO Andy Grove's famous personal motto: "Only the paranoid survive."[58]

Looking Forward to Future Exchange

Experience teaches that there are no cookie-cutter methods for strategic management. A solution can only succeed if it is tailored to a specific organizational and strategic context. Efforts to graft existing "best practice" wholesale from one organization to another often fail because success hinges on micro-level incentives and cultural expectations as much as on grand vision and formal processes. Many have tried to duplicate Shell's scenario successes, but few have succeeded.[59] For similar reasons, Toyota does not fear opening its plants up to public tours because its leadership understands that copying its explicit processes and operational procedures alone cannot replicate the famed Toyota Production System.

This survey of private sector experience, though, suggests ten themes relevant to the future of foreign policy planning:

1. "Real strategy is made in real time."[60] Strategy is made from decisions and actions, not plans.

2. Reality intrudes. Most decisions with strategic impact are made outside of a formal strategic planning calendar.

3. Strategies evolve, therefore, over time and involve both deliberate and emergent elements.

4. Strategic planning should be about learning and adapting, not about the plans themselves. Planning should help "prepare minds" and the organization to make the right decisions and then execute when opportunities arise.

5. Consider experimenting with formal or informal dialogue on selected strategic topics separate from regular annual planning or budgeting processes. Current and near-term operational and financial performance naturally captures leaders' attention, thereby crowding out consideration of long-term, strategic issues.

6. Strategic planning is one side of the coin, execution the other. Both are essential. Success requires, therefore, a comprehensive approach to *strategic management*.

7. The CEO must "own" the strategy. He or she must talk the talk *and* walk the walk for a strategic management system to function.

8. Executives and operators make strategy come to life; they must be involved throughout the strategy development process.

9. Planners do not make strategy; they should help those who do.

10. No one should be complacent. Strategy is a never ending race.

These themes do not provide easy answers to improve foreign policy planning; rather, they help frame hard questions for those responsible for managing the process in the future. Will the president and his Cabinet officers make strategic management of our national security policy a top priority in word and deed? Should the national security adviser or someone else play a CSO role in the White House? What steps should be taken to communicate a serious commitment to strategic management that could influence conduct throughout the sprawling national security bureaucracy? What mechanisms could ensure the accountability needed to keep a strategy process on track? What additional staff might be needed? Are changes needed in personnel policies? What forum could bring together senior leadership with skilled implementers for serious dialogue about strategic challenges? Should existing policy planning staffs take on the role of internal consultants? Or should alternative approaches to build internal policy planning capabilities be considered? What information technology and knowledge management investments are needed to manage strategy in real time?

Many of these themes from private sector experience should have a familiar sound to practitioners of foreign policy. The best operators know instinctively that they also must be policy planners. The theme of "prepared minds" echoes Dwight Eisenhower's famous observation that "plans are useless . . . planning is indispensable."[61] George Kennan's lament about his policy planning staff's ineffectiveness because of its separation from line responsibilities would sound familiar to most corporate vice presidents of strategy. And digging deeper into the history of statecraft, we have Cardinal Richelieu's warning: "Those who work for the king must remember that there is a great difference between simply ordering what needs to be done and getting the orders carried out. One must take care not to be satisfied with merely giving orders, for everything lies in the execution of them."[62] The cardinal did not need the *Harvard Business Review* to teach that lesson! Despite differences, planning in the private and public sectors share many of the same timeless challenges because they arise from human nature and our limitations, how we organize, and the inherent uncertainties involved when we must decide and act.

This chapter's modest goal is to demonstrate that strategic planning commerce across the private-public boundary is both practical and valuable. This trade could be expanded to include specific tactics for effective strategic management (meeting preparation, metric design, and others), analytic techniques to support the strategy process, and the cognitive foundations for innovation and strategy development. There is every reason to believe, moreover, that future trade across this border can flow in both directions. Perhaps the private and public sectors are not so different after all.

Notes

1. In his final months in office, President George W. Bush approved a National Security Presidential Directive that formally established an interagency strategic planning committee. It remains to be seen whether this seed will take root and blossom.

2. See, for instance, Lincoln P. Bloomfield, "Planning Foreign Policy: Can It Be Done?" *Political Science Quarterly* (Autumn 1978): 369–91; Andrew Bennett and Bruce Jentleson, "Policy Planning: Oxymoron or Sine Qua Non for U.S. Foreign Policy?" in *Good Judgment in Foreign Policy: Theory and Application,* edited by Deborah Larson and Stanley Renshon (Lanham, Md.: Rowman & Littlefield, 2002), pp. 219–45; Aaron L. Friedberg, "Strengthening U.S. Strategic Planning," *Washington Quarterly* (Winter 2007/08): 47–60. Author's interviews with Bush administration officials involved in interagency policy planning process, 2008. The primary exception to this observation is the adoption of scenario planning techniques originally developed in the private sector. Peter Schwartz, *The Art of the Long View: Planning for the Future in an Uncertain*

World (New York: Currency, 1996). For an example of the application of scenario techniques by the U.S. intelligence community, see National Intelligence Council, *Global Trends 2025: A Transformed World* (Washington: GPO, 2008) (www.dni.gov/nic/NIC_2025_project.html [January 2009]).

3. The exception was Paul Nitze, the second director of the policy planning staff (1950–53). His first career was as a Wall Street investment banker.

4. Richard N. Haass, *The Bureaucratic Entrepreneur: How to Be Effective in Any Unruly Organization* (Washington: Brookings, 1999), esp. pp. 7–14; Laurence E. Lynn Jr., *Managing the Public's Business: The Job of the Government Executive* (New York: Basic Books, 1981), esp. pp. 103–37.

5. James Steinberg, comments at "The Past, Present, and Future of Policy Planning" conference, Fletcher School, Tufts University, April 17, 2008.

6. See Richard N. Haass's observations in Andrew Erdmann, Roger C. Kline, and Lenny T. Mendonca, "A Political Education for Business: An Interview with the Head of the Council on Foreign Relations," *McKinsey Quarterly* (February 2008) (www.mckinsey quarterly.com/Governance/A_political_education_for_business_An_interview_with_ the_head_of_the_Council_on_Foreign_Relations_21 [October 2008]).

7. For an overview of the development of the strategy field and its main schools of thought, see *The Oxford Handbook of Strategy*, 2 vols., edited by David O. Falkner and Andrew Campbell (Oxford University Press, 2003); Pankaj Ghemawat, "Competition and Business Strategy in Historical Perspective," *Business History Review* (Spring 2002): 37–74; Giovanni Gavetti and Daniel A. Levinthal, "The Strategy Field from the Perspective of *Management Science:* Divergent Strands and Possible Integration," *Management Science* (October 2004): 1309–18; Henry Mintzberg, *The Rise and Fall of Strategic Planning* (New York: Free Press, 1994); Henry Mintzberg, Bruce Ahlstrand, and Joseph Lampel, *Strategy Safari: A Guided Tour through the Wilds of Strategic Management* (New York: Free Press, 1998); Andrew Pettigrew, Howard Thomas, and Richard Whittington, eds., *Handbook of Strategy and Management* (London: Sage, 2006); Michael E. Porter, "What Is Strategy?" *Harvard Business Review* (November–December 1996): 61–78; Michael E. Porter, "The Five Competitive Forces That Shape Strategy," *Harvard Business Review* (January 2008): 79–93; Richard P. Rumelt, Dan E. Schendel, and David J. Teece, *Fundamental Issues in Strategy: A Research Agenda* (Harvard Business School Press, 1994).

8. Christopher A. Bartlett and Meg Wozny, "GE's Two-Decade Transformation: Jack Welch's Leadership," Case 9-399-150 (Harvard Business School, 2005), p. 2.

9. Darrell Rigby, "Management Tools and Trends 2007" (Bain and Company, 2007) (www.bain.com/management_tools/Management_Tools_and_Trends_2007.pdf [October 2008]). In a survey, Bain defined strategic planning as: "a comprehensive process for determining what a business should become and how it can best achieve that goal. It appraises the full potential of a business and explicitly links the business's objectives to the actions and resources required to achieve them. Strategic Planning offers a systematic process to ask and answer the most critical questions

confronting a management team—especially large, irrevocable resource commitment decisions." See www.bain.com/management_tools/tools_planning.asp?groupcode=2 [October 2008].

10. Larry Bossidy and Ram Charan, *Execution: The Discipline of Getting Things Done* (New York: Crown Business, 2002); Charles F. Knight and Davis Dyer, *Performance without Compromise: How Emerson Consistently Achieves Winning Results* (Harvard Business School Press, 2005).

11. Quoted in Richard N. Foster and Sarah Kaplan, *Creative Destruction: Why Companies That Are Built to Last Underperform the Market—and How to Successfully Transform Them* (New York: Currency, 2001), pp. 211–12.

12. Quoted in Sarah Kaplan and Eric D. Beinhocker, "The Real Value of Strategic Planning," *Sloan Management Review* (Winter 2003): 71.

13. Jack Welch with John A. Byrne, *Jack: Straight from the Gut* (New York: Warner Books, 2003), p. 93.

14. Michael C. Mankins and Richard Steele, "Stop Making Plans; Start Making Decisions," *Harvard Business Review* (January 2006) (Harvard Business School OnPoint reprint), p. 8.

15. Renée Dye and Olivier Sibony, "How to Improve Strategic Planning," *McKinsey Quarterly,* no. 3 (2007): 40.

16. Mankins and Steele, "Stop Making Plans," pp. 4–8; Joseph L. Bower and Clark G. Gilbert, "How Managers' Everyday Decisions Create or Destroy Your Company's Strategy," *Harvard Business Review* (February 2007): 72–79.

17. "Improving Strategic Planning: A McKinsey Survey" (September 2006), Exhibits 1 and 2 (www.mckinseyquarterly.com/PDFDownload.aspx?L2=21&L3=0&ar=1819 [October 2008]). See also "McKinsey Global Survey Results: How Companies Make Good Decisions," *McKinsey Quarterly* (December 2008), Exhibit 2 (www.mckinsey quarterly.com/PDFDownload.aspx?L2=21&L3=37&ar=2282 [January 2009]).

18. Ibid., Exhibit 5.

19. "Better Strategy for Business Units: A McKinsey Survey," *McKinsey Quarterly* (July 2007), Exhibit 2 (www.mckinseyquarterly.com/PDFDownload.aspx?L2= 21&L3=37&ar=2038 [October 2008]); "How Companies Respond to Competitors: A McKinsey Global Survey," *McKinsey Quarterly* (April 2008) (www.mckinseyquarterly. com/PDFDownload.aspx?L2=21&L3=37&ar=2146 [January 2009]). In another survey, only 14 percent replied that they were "consistently presented with alternative strategies." Michael C. Mankins, "Stop Wasting Valuable Time," *Harvard Business Review* (September 2004), in *Great Strategy and Great Results,* 2nd ed. (*Harvard Business Review* article reprint collection, 2008), p. 60.

20. Henry Mintzberg, "The Fall and Rise of Strategic Planning," *Harvard Business Review* (January–February 1994): 107–14.

21. Mankins and Steele, "Stop Making Plans," p. 6.

22. Michael Mankins, "Making Strategy Development Matter," *Harvard Management Update* (May 2004).

23. Henry Mintzberg, *Tracking Strategies . . . Toward a General Theory* (Oxford University Press, 2007), pp. 1–16. The quotation is from Herbert Simon's *Model of Man* (New York: Wiley, 1957), p. 67. In the late 1990s, some consultants embraced a definition of strategy that could accommodate emergent strategy development: "Strategy is a handful of decisions that drive or shape most of a company's subsequent actions, are not easily changed once made, and have the greatest impact on whether a company meets its strategic objectives." See Kevin P. Coyne and Somu Subramaniam, "Bringing Discipline to Strategy," *McKinsey Quarterly* (June 2000) (www.mckinseyquarterly.com/Bringing_discipline_to_strategy_1054 (October 2008)].

24. Amar Bhide, *The Origin and Evolution of New Businesses* (Oxford University Press, 2000).

25. Quoted in Eric D. Beinhocker, *The Origin of Wealth: The Radical Remaking of Economics and What It Means for Business and Society* (Harvard Business School Press, 2006), p. 348.

26. Richard T. Pascale, "Perspectives on Strategy: The Real Story behind Honda's Success," *California Management Review* (Spring 1984): 47–72.

27. Henry Mintzberg and James A. Waters, "Of Strategies, Deliberate and Emergent," *Strategic Management Journal* (July–September 1985): 271.

28. Jan W. Rivkin, "Where Do Successful Strategies Come From?" Teaching Note 9-706-432 (Harvard Business School, 2005), p. 4.

29. Eric D. Beinhocker and Sarah Kaplan, "Tired of Strategic Planning?" *McKinsey Quarterly* (2002 Special Edition: Risk and Resilience): 51, emphasis in original.

30. Kaplan and Beinhocker, "The Real Value of Strategic Planning," pp. 71–76, quotation from p. 71. See also Arie de Geus, "Planning as Learning," *Harvard Business Review* (March–April 1988): 70–74.

31. On the development of scenario planning at Royal Dutch/Shell Group, see Peter Cornelius, Alexander van de Putte, and Mattia Romani, "Three Decades of Scenario Planning in Shell," *California Management Review* (Fall 2005): 92–109; Art Kleiner, "The Man Who Saw the Future," *Strategy + Business* (Spring 2003) (www.strategy-business.com/press/16635507/8220 [October 2008]); Schwartz, *The Art of the Long View,* esp. p. 9, regarding the executive-scenario planner partnership; Pierre Wack, "Scenarios: Uncharted Waters Ahead," *Harvard Business Review* (September–October 1985): 73–89; Pierre Wack, "Scenarios: Shooting the Rapids," *Harvard Business Review* (November–December 1985): 139–50, quotation from p. 140; Ian Wylie, "There Is No Alternative to . . . ," *FastCompany* (June 2002) (www.fastcompany.com/magazine/60/tina.html [October 2008]). On Shell's recent scenario work, see Royal Dutch/Shell Group, *Shell Global Scenarios to 2025—The Future Business Environment: Trends, Trade-offs and Choices* (Royal Dutch/Shell Group, 2005), and its scenario website, www.shell.com/home/content/aboutshell/our_strategy/shell_global_scenarios/dir_global_scenarios_07112006.html [October 2008]. Regarding potential limitations of scenarios, see Philip E. Tetlock, *Expert Political Judgment: How Good Is It? How Do We Know?* (Princeton University Press, 2005), pp. 189–215.

32. Quoted in Thomas F. O'Boyle, *At Any Cost: Jack Welch, General Electric, and the Pursuit of Profit* (New York: Knopf, 1998), p. 68.

33. Bartlett and Wozny, "GE's Two-Decade Transformation," 2, 9; O'Boyle, *At Any Cost*, pp. 67–70; Welch, *Straight from the Gut*. For a graphic representation of General Electric's "Operating System," see Noel M. Tichy and Warren G. Bennis, *Judgment: How Wining Leaders Make Great Calls* (New York: Portfolio, 2007), pp. 250–51.

34. Ralph S. Larson, "FrameworkS: An Innovative Process for Turning the Challenges of Change into Opportunities for Growth," *CEO Series*, no. 21 (Center for the Study of American Business, Washington University, 1998); Foster and Kaplan, *Creative Destruction*, pp. 261–87.

35. Gary Hamel with Bill Breen, *The Future of Management* (Harvard Business School Press, 2007), pp. 101–21, quotations from pp. 110, 113. For an evolutionary conception of business strategy development, see Beinhocker, *The Origin of Wealth*, pp. 323–48.

36. Mankins, "Stop Wasting Valuable Time"; Mankins and Steele. "Stop Making Plans."

37. Dan P. Lovella and Lenny T. Mendonca, "Strategy's Strategist: An Interview with Richard Rumelt," *McKinsey Quarterly* (November 2007), (www.mckinseyquarterly.com/Strategys_strategist_An_interview_with_Richard_Rumelt_2039 [October 2008]).

38. Dye and Sibony, "How to Improve Strategic Planning," pp. 43–45. For an introduction to the range of analytic tools to support strategic planning, tailored to different environments, see Hugh Courtney, *20/20 Foresight: Crafting Strategy in an Uncertain World* (Harvard Business School Press, 2001).

39. Robert Bowie, "Planning in the Department," *Foreign Service Journal* (March 1961): 22.

40. Robert S. Kaplan and David P. Norton, "Mastering the Management System," *Harvard Business Review* (January 2008): 64.

41. Andrew Campbell and Marcus Alexander, "What's Wrong with Strategy?" *Harvard Business Review* (November–December 1997): 2–8.

42. Frederick W. Gluck, Stephen P. Kaufman, and A. Steven Walleck, "The Evolution of Strategic Management," McKinsey & Company Staff Paper (1978), excerpt published in *McKinsey Quarterly Anthology: On Strategy* (2000): 10–16.

43. For an excellent synthesis of recent strategic management literature, see Kaplan and Norton, "Mastering the Management System," pp. 63–77.

44. Bartlett and Wozny, "GE's Two-Decade Transformation"; Jacqueline Durett, "GE Hones Its Leaders at Crotonville," *Training*, May 1, 2006 (www.allbusiness.com/services/educational-services/4285722-1.html [October 2008]); Welch, *Straight from the Gut*.

45. In January 2008, twenty-six GE alumni were CEOs of top 1,187 publicly traded U.S. companies, for a ratio of one CEO for every 11,540 employees. The management consultancy McKinsey & Company was the top CEO-producing firm in terms of ratio—one CEO for every 690 employees. Del Jones, "Some Firms' Fertile Soil Grows

Crops of CEOs," *USA Today,* January 9, 2008 (www.usatoday.com/money/companies/management/2008-01-08-ceo-companies_n.htm [October 2008]).

46. David E. Bell, "Tesco PLC," Case 9-503-036 (Harvard Business School Press, 2003); Rhys Blakely, "Revealed: The Secret of Tesco's Success," *Times Online,* October 18, 2004 (www.business.timesonline.co.uk/tol/business/industry_sectors/retailing/article496014.ece [October 2008]); Sue Grist, "Driving Performance with Balanced Scorecard," *M & C Report* (June 2005), pp. 8–9 (www.egremontgroup.com/fileadmin/Site_Files/Articles/Balanced_Scorecard_M_C_Report_June_2005.pdf [January 2009]); Clive Humbly, Terry Hunt, and Tim Phillips, *Scoring Points: How Tesco Continues to Win Customer Loyalty,* 2nd ed. (London: Kogan Page, 2007); *Tesco PLC Annual Report and Financial Statement 2008* and *Tesco PLC Corporate Social Responsibility Report 2008* (for "Steering Wheel," see p. 48). Both accessed at (www.tescoreports.com/ [October 2008]). On "balanced scorecards," see Robert S. Kaplan and David P. Norton, *The Balanced Scorecard: Translating Strategy into Action* (Harvard Business School Press, 1996); Robert S. Kaplan and David P. Norton, *The Strategy-Focused Organization: How Balanced Scorecard Companies Thrive in the New Business Environment* (Harvard Business School Press, 2001); Robert S. Kaplan and David P. Norton, *Alignment: Using the Balanced Scorecard to Create Corporate Synergies* (Harvard Business School Press, 2006).

47. Three examples: First, less than 15 percent of companies regularly compare performance to the previous year's strategic plan forecast. See Michael C. Mankins and Richard Steele, "Turning Great Strategy into Great Performance," *Harvard Business Review* (July–August 2005) [Harvard Business School OnPoint reprint], p. 3. Second, compensation for 90 percent of frontline workers has no connection to strategy execution. Third, 95 percent of a typical company's workforce is not aware of or does not understand its strategy. See Robert S. Kaplan and David P. Norton, "Office of Strategy Management," *Harvard Business Review* (October 2005) [Harvard Business School OnPoint reprint], pp. 2–3.

48. Emerson acquired more than 200 companies from around the world to fuel its growth during Chuck Knight's tenure as CEO. All eventually assimilated Emerson's distinctive strategic management system, although the process would take normally at least one year. R. Michael Murray Jr. and Warren L. Strickland, "Managing for Growth: An Interview with Former Emerson CEO Chuck Knight," *McKinsey Quarterly* (November 2006) (www.mckinseyquarterly.com/Managing_for_growth_An_interview_with_former_Emerson_CEO_Chuck_Knight_1876 [October 2008]).

49. Most corporate change efforts fail to achieve their objectives. For a classic diagnosis, see John P. Kotter, "Leading Change: Why Transformation Efforts Fail," *Harvard Business Review* (March–April 1995): 59–67. On the CEO's critical role, see Cynthia A. Montgomery, "Putting Leadership Back into Strategy," *Harvard Business Review* (January 2008): 54–60.

50. Bower and Gilbert, "How Managers' Everyday Decisions Create or Destroy Your Company's Strategy"; Campbell and Alexander, "What's Wrong with Strategy?";

Dye and Sibony, "How to Improve Strategic Planning," pp. 43–44; Beinhocker and Kaplan, "Tired of Strategic Planning?" p. 53.

51. Mintzberg, "The Fall and Rise of Strategic Planning," p. 108, emphasis in original.

52. Beinhocker and Kaplan, "Tired of Strategic Planning?" pp. 56–57, quotation from p. 56; "Improving Strategic Planning: A McKinsey Survey," p. 9; Robert S. Kaplan and David P. Norton, "The Office of Strategic Management," *Harvard Business Review* (October 2005): 72–80; Mintzberg, "The Fall and Rise of Strategic Planning"; Mintzberg, *The Rise and Fall of Strategic Planning*.

53. Robert S. Kaplan and David P. Norton, "Strategic Management: An Emerging Profession," *Balance Scorecard Update* (May–June 2004).

54. Renée Dye, "How Chief Strategy Officers Think about Their Role: A Round-table," *McKinsey Quarterly* (May 2008) (www.mckinseyquarterly.com/Strategy/Strategy_in_Practice/How_chief_strategy_officers_think_about_their_role_A_roundtable_2143 [October 2008]).

55. R. Timothy S. Breene, Paul F. Nunes, and Walter E. Shill, "The Chief Strategy Officer," *Harvard Business Review* (October 2007): 84–93; Tim Breene, Paul Nunes, and Walt Shill, "Rise of the Chief Strategy Officer," *Outlook* (January 2008) (www.accenture.com/Global/Research_and_Insights/Outlook/By_Issue/Y2008/RiseoftheCSO.htm [October 2008]).

56. A similar indicator of the challenges of survival: of the 1957 Standard & Poor's (S&P) 500, only seventy-four remained in 1997, and just twelve outperformed the S&P Index over that period. Foster and Kaplan, *Creative Destruction*, pp. 7–8; Beinhocker, *The Origin of Wealth*, pp. 332–33. See also Phil Rosenzweig, *The Halo Effect . . . and Eight Other Business Delusions That Deceive Managers* (New York: Free Press, 2007), pp. 101–05.

57. The Red Queen said, "In this place it takes all the running you can do, to keep in the same place." Beinhocker, *The Origin of Wealth*, pp. 323–48, quotations from p. 332. See also Rosenzweig, *The Halo Effect*, pp. 101–05, 142–74.

58. Andy S. Grove, *Only the Paranoid Survive: How to Exploit Crisis Points That Challenge Every Company* (New York: Doubleday, 1999). See also Robert A. Burgel-man, *Strategy Is Destiny: How Strategy-Making Shapes a Company's Future* (New York: Free Press, 2002).

59. As Peter Schwartz has concluded, "Many of the people using scenarios are doing so in a trivial way with little impact." Quoted in Wylie, "There Is No Alternative to . . ."

60. Kaplan and Beinhocker, "The Real Value of Strategic Planning," p. 72.

61. Eisenhower quoted in Richard Nixon, *Six Crises* (Garden City, N.J.: Doubleday, 1962), p. 235. See also Friedberg, "Strengthening U.S. Strategic Planning."

62. Quoted in J. H. Elliott, *Richelieu and Olivares* (Cambridge University Press, 1984), p. 132.

STEPHEN D. KRASNER

11

The Garbage Can Framework
for Locating Policy Planning

Foreign policy is a particularly complex arena. There are many different actors—not just states, but also international and regional organizations, transnational groups both benign and malign, multinational corporations, domestic interest groups, NGOs, and others. The capacity of these different actors may be difficult to assess. Their motivations may be opaque. Principals have to weigh not only the domestic political reaction in the United States to foreign policy initiatives, but also the constraints confronting their counterparts in other countries.

Paul Nitze wrote in 1954, when he was director of policy planning:

> To deal with such problems as present themselves to S/P [the State Department designation for the policy planning office] in the full richness of their reality would require methods analogous to the simultaneous solution of an almost infinite series of equations in the higher calculus. Many of the problems are without clear precedent; they cannot be resolved solely on the basis of tradition or of historical experience. The question is not whether to use the tools of political theory and political philosophy. The question is rather what tools are applicable to what situations and to what end.[1]

Even in benign periods, principals have limited time. Every appointment, every phone call, has an opportunity cost. Blink capacity, the ability to get the right answer without spending too much time thinking about it, is critical.[2] Within this environment what role has policy planning played and can it play?

No policy planning director has been ignorant of what many still consider the peak achievement of strategic planning, George Kennan's idea of containment. Of course, containment was first presented in the Long Telegram, which Kennan sent from Moscow where he was stationed as a foreign service officer. The policy planning staff did not exist when Kennan wrote his message. The actual implementation of containment was very different from Kennan's original ideas. Perhaps since containment had little to do with the policy planning bureau, it is not surprising that Kennan's accomplishment has not been replicated.

In practice the policy planning staff at the State Department does a number of different things, including writing memos for the secretary, clearing on at least most of the papers that are sent to principals on the seventh floor (where the offices of the secretary, deputy secretary, under secretary for political affairs, several assistant secretaries, and policy planning are located), engaging with the secretary's speechwriters, developing specific policy initiatives, and conducting dialogues with counterpart staffs around the world. Is the planning staff useful? Sometimes. Memos to the secretary sometimes stick, but often do not, like spaghetti thrown against the wall. Policy initiatives that begin in policy planning can be successful, but only if they are ultimately carried out by an operational bureau. Speechwriters sit in the policy planning office, but they work directly for the secretary, and they might, or might not, use input from the policy planning staff. Policy planning dialogues with counterpart agencies in other countries and organizations can facilitate understanding, especially because they do not have to focus on operational outcomes, but they can also be a waste of time.

There are a lot of smart people in the American government, and policy planning is only one office where they are housed. Policy planning does have one luxury that is not enjoyed by other bureaus: time to think. Its staff has also had a more diverse background than other staffs in the State Department, with members coming from the permanent bureaucracy, the Foreign Service, and outside government. It suffers, however, from one major deficit: it does not have operational capacity. It can frame ideas but it cannot on its own implement them.

Could the policy planning function within the State Department, and the U.S. government more generally, be improved by changing the organizational structure? I am skeptical. The foreign policymaking process is best captured by the imaginatively named "garbage can model" of decisionmaking first developed by Michael Cohen, James March, and Johan Olsen in the early 1970s and then elaborated by John Kingdon in his idea of policy streams.

Cohen, March, and Olsen applied their model to what they called "organized anarchies," organizations with shifting actors, problematic preferences, and trial-and-error decisionmaking.[3] In organized anarchies, outcomes are the result of the convergence of problems, solutions, people, and choice opportunities. Individual actors attach solutions to problems. These actors do not necessarily have consistent preference orderings. Relevant actors change over time and across issue areas. Problems may have access to many possible solutions or to few. Higher-level decisionmakers have access to more solutions, but less time. Lower-level officials, charged with dealing with a specific problem, have more time but fewer solutions available to them.

Cohen, March, and Olsen summarize their position in the following way:

> From this point of view, an organization is a collection of choices looking for problems, issues and feelings looking for decision situations in which they might be aired, solutions looking for issues to which they might be the answer, and decision makers looking for work....
>
> To understand processes within organizations, one can view a choice opportunity as a garbage can into which various kinds of problems and solutions are dumped by participants as they are generated. The mix of garbage in a single can depends on the mix of cans available, on the labels attached to the alternative cans, on what garbage is currently being produced, and on the speed with which garbage is collected and removed from the scene[4]

John Kingdon reframes the garbage can model.[5] Although Kingdon focuses on agenda setting, his framework can be applied to the entire policy process.[6] Empirically, Kingdon's study, the first edition of which was published in 1984, was based largely on data collected in the 1970s and focused on two issues, health care and transportation. Kingdon's framework treats the U.S. national government as an organized anarchy. Preferences may be opaque or contradictory. Actors move in and out of the policy process. There are disagreements among agencies and bureaus. Jurisdictional boundaries are not clear. Technologies are uncertain; it is not clear how inputs into a process are turned into outputs. A particular military strategy, for instance, might, or might not, be successfully implemented; and even if it is implemented successfully it might, or might not, accomplish its stated objective. Given uncertain preferences, changing actors, and unproven technologies, past experiences often guide action, and trial and error is inevitable. Fully rational decisionmaking in which principals assess all policy options and choose the one that maximizes their utility is impossible for all of the familiar reasons.

There are five components to Kingdon's framework: three policy streams and two factors that can bring the streams together. The three streams—policy recognition, policy alternatives, and politics—flow more or less independently. Each has its own dynamic. Policy windows, where the three streams can be joined to create new initiatives, can be consciously opened by policy entrepreneurs or politicians, or thrown open by crises, such as 9/11 or Katrina. When a policy window does open, change can be dramatic, not just incremental.

Problem recognition transforms an issue from a condition to a problem. A condition is something that cannot or need not be changed. A problem is something that policymakers must address. If health care is regarded as a right, Kingdon observes, it is a problem that needs to be dealt with. If health care is not regarded as a right, then it is a condition that policymakers can neglect.[7] If the absence of democracy in the Middle East is irrelevant for American economic and security interests, then it is a condition that can be ignored; if the absence of democracy in the Middle East generates transnational terrorism that threatens the national security of the United States, it is a problem that must be confronted.

Problem recognition occurs for a variety of reasons. There may be crises, dramatic and unforeseen events that demand a response. Alternatively, indicators, especially quantitative indicators and other kinds of feedback, may reveal that a policy is not accomplishing its intended objectives. Bureaucrats trying to expand their turf may attempt to transform a condition into a problem. Politicians may try to make their mark by identifying a problem. Lobbying groups, striving to further their interests, may attempt to raise the saliency of an issue.[8]

The second stream, policy alternatives, is moved by very different currents. Policy alternatives are cooked up by policy communities in what Kingdon refers to as the "policy primeval soup."[9] Policy communities exist inside and outside of government. They are composed of experts, including academics, think tank professionals, congressional staff members, and bureaucrats.

Policy planning staffs are part of the policy alternatives stream. One of their primary missions is to develop solutions that can be attached to problems. They have unique advantages over other actors in this stream. They have access to high officials. In the case of policy planning at the State Department, the director may have the opportunity to sit in on small daily meetings that the secretary holds with close staff and to travel with the secretary. Close access means not only the opportunity to put something in front of the secretary, but also knowledge of those issues that the secretary is most deeply concerned about at any particular moment.

Policy alternatives are more likely to survive, Kingdon asserts, if they are well cooked. A new proposal is more likely to result from recombining well-understood existing ideas than from a completely new approach not previously considered. A policy proposals has to be technically feasible—not only a good idea that could work, but a good idea that can be effectively implemented and administered. To have any chance of success, policy proposals also have to conform with the ideology of policymakers. Persuasion, Kingdon argues, is the coin of the realm in the policy alternatives stream. Over time, a consensus may develop if the proponents of a particular approach are persuasive enough.

In an interesting amendment to Kindgon's original position, Robert Durant and Paul Diehl suggest that the cooking may be less thorough in the foreign policy arena.[10] In making foreign policy, the president, as the key political actor in the United States, operates with fewer constraints and in a more hierarchical way than in domestic policymaking. As commander-in-chief the president has constitutional prerogatives in the national security arena that have no domestic equivalent. The president can rely on a small number of close advisers, including the secretaries of state and defense, the national security adviser, and the vice president. The president can also establish counter-bureaucracies in the White House that can circumvent established agencies. In the policy stream, officials in the White House or specifically designated bureaucracies may generate alternatives that have not been well cooked within some larger policy community. The president and his close advisers may have privileged information in the foreign policy arena that is available only to a limited number of players in both the policy alternatives and the political streams. Foreign policy crises may demand action even if there is no well-cooked policy alternative available.

Politics is the third stream that enters into the policy process. The political stream, like the problem recognition and policy alternative streams, moves according to its own logic. The main elements affecting the flow of the political stream are: the national mood, interest group campaigns, and administrative or legislative turnover. Politicians are interested in staying in office. They are attentive to the national mood, to sentiments that they might attach to particular policy initiatives. They may be moved by interest group pressure or by communications from constituents. Attentiveness to particular problems can shift, depending on which individuals hold positions of power. Such changes take place when a new administration begins and hundreds, even thousands, of offices change hands. They may also take place when committee chairs change or when new appointees assume important positions in the bureaucracy.[11]

In the political stream, consensus is built primarily through bargaining rather than persuasion. Politicians are interested in different issues. They may be able to link issues in ways that push their own agenda items. If a particular initiative catches on, many politicians will try to jump on the bandwagon.

The problem recognition, policy alternatives, and political streams flow along independent of each other. Sometimes a great policy alternative exists, but no politician is interested in the associated problem. Sometimes a serious problem exists but with no available feasible policy alternatives. A politician may be interested in a specific problem, but no policy alternative exists that is consistent with that politician's ideological orientation.[12]

The streams come together when a policy window opens. (The mixed metaphor here is Kingdon's, not mine.) Sometimes policy windows open for predictable reasons—for instance, a piece of legislation must be renewed, or a new administration takes office. Sometimes they open because of a dramatic and unpredicted external event like 9/11. Sometimes policy windows are opened by policy entrepreneurs, individuals who are well connected and knowledgeable. Policy entrepreneurs are familiar with what is going on in all three streams, with what kind of garbage is in the available garbage cans at any particular moment. They are most likely to be effective when they have direct access to politicians in the political stream, a privileged position that some policy planning directors in government enjoy.

In foreign affairs some policy windows can stay open for years. War fighting is one example. In other foreign policy arenas, however, the opportunities for policy change are short lived. The public mood can cause leading politicians to distance themselves from a problem. When new leaders arrive, they bring with them different agendas. A policy entrepreneur capable of linking policy alternatives with problems might lose favor.

In sum, the multiple-streams framework provides a way of thinking about how policy planning staffs, one part of the policy alternatives stream, can influence policy. Policy planning staffs have unusual advantages because they combine access with the ability to think strategically. But these advantages are not unique. There are individuals and bureaus throughout the government with the same capacity. Policy planning staffs will never be the only entities in the government engaged in strategic planning.

Two Examples

Two examples from my own experience at the State Department illustrate how the policy streams model can provide a framework for understanding how the policy planning staff can contribute to policy initiatives. The first, challenging China to be a responsible stakeholder, involves a classic example of providing a conceptual framework for policy. A successful framework will almost certainly capture a least some things that the government is already doing. For instance, the United States was already engaged in containment by the time the containment doctrine was accepted; it was deterring before deterrence was explicitly recognized as a guide for policy. A successful framework must also have heuristic punch. It must provide guidance for policy over a range of specific issues, some of which might not even be explicitly recognized when the conceptualization was first articulated. Finally, a successful framework must work; that is, it must point to a coherent set of specific initiatives that can be successfully implemented and achieve their objective.

The second example, the Partnership for Democratic Governance, involves a specific policy initiative, an activity that policy planning staffs have sometimes but not always engaged in. Success here depends not only on getting support from principals, but also on lining up bureaucratic allies who must ultimately implement an initiative once it is adopted.

Conceptual Framing: China as a Responsible Stakeholder

In a speech to the National Committee on U.S.-China Relations in September 2005, Robert Zoellick, the deputy secretary of state, urged China to be a "responsible stakeholder" in the international system. Zoellick went on to say: "From China's perspective, it would seem that its national interest would be much better served by working with us to shape the future international system."[13] Zoellick noted that many major international issues, including transnational terrorism, disease, the proliferation of weapons of mass destruction, and poverty, could be more effectively addressed if China and the United States were cooperating with each other. He contrasted the American relationships with contemporary China and the Soviet Union during the cold war, noting that China was not committed to overturning the existing international system, or to an implacable ideological struggle with the United States, or to capitalism. He stated that nineteenth-century balance-of-power concepts were outmoded in the contemporary globalized world. He argued that China, to successfully address its domestic problems (notably rural poverty), needed a benign international environment. He then pointed out a number of Chinese policies that were problematic, including insufficient transparency in its military budget, theft of intellectual property, growing mercantilism, and efforts to "lock up" oil supplies through reliance on equity investments instead of the market, and contrasted them with policies of engagement such as the Six-Party Talks and foreign assistance pledges for Afghanistan and Iraq. He urged China to do more to resolve the crisis in Sudan, to work cooperatively for security in Asia, and to correct its own historical blind spots. He argued that greater democratization would be necessary for China's own growth and stability. Zoellick concluded by stating:

> Tonight I have suggested that the U.S. response should be to help foster constructive action by transforming our thirty-year policy of integration: We now need to encourage China to become a responsible stakeholder in the international system. As a responsible stakeholder, China would be more than just a member—it would work with us to sustain the international system that has enabled its success.

The conceptualization of China as a responsible stakeholder went beyond the notion of engagement that had been used by six previous administrations and that focused in large part on domestic change within China. Zoellick argued that China was failing to act in its own self-interest as the Chinese regime itself had defined it because China's "peaceful rise" would be impossible without a stable international system, and a stable international system would be more difficult to sustain if China were not playing by—and then working to support, sustain, and adapt—the rules. Although Zoellick did not use the term "free rider," which for diplomatic discourse might have been either too wonky or too provocative, the danger for China of China's free riding was exactly what the speech was about. Indeed, Zoellick noted that the U.S. administration would not be able to continue to run interference for China in Congress without a change in China's behavior.

Evan Feigenbaum, who was then responsible for Asia on the policy planning staff, played an important role in developing responsible stakeholder as a frame for organizing American policy toward China. Feigenbaum had written a memo for Secretary of State Colin Powell in 2002 about China in which he used the phrase "constructive stakeholder," followed by a transition memo for Secretary Condoleezza Rice in which the words responsible and stakeholder were prominent, although they were not placed right next to each other, arguing that China should be challenged to "assume the responsibilities of a stakeholder" in the international system. These memos had been sent to principals and others on the seventh floor. They had no impact on policy. Feigenbaum had proposed a solution to a problem that none of the relevant principals were focusing on.

When Zoellick arrived at the State Department in February of 2005, he made it clear that China was one of the areas that he would be particularly attentive to. He expressed an interest in meeting with the policy planning staff, and after several tries an opening was found on his schedule. (Spending forty-five minutes without trying to reach agreement on a specific policy question is a significant opportunity cost for the deputy secretary of state, so it came as no surprise that scheduling the meeting took some time.) Feigenbaum had an exceptional command of the facts, and he could conceptualize problems in ways that were useful to policymakers. I am sure that the contribution that Feigenbaum could make to China policy was immediately apparent to Zoellick, as the members of the staff went around the room describing their responsibilities.

Zoellick enlisted Feigenbaum to work with him on China policy. One of the first things that Feigenbaum did, at Zoellick's request, was to pull his old memo out of the drawer, tidy it up a bit so that Zoellick could use it with the secretary and others, and give it a new date. Zoellick and his principal speech-writer then put the words "responsible" and "stakeholder" right next to each other in a draft of a speech. Before the speech was made, Zoellick engaged in extensive private discussions with some of his Chinese counterparts, as well as with China experts in the United States. He then deployed the phrase no fewer than five times in the text.

The Chinese took the challenge of being a responsible stakeholder seriously. They were initially at pains to understand what the term meant. The Chinese ambassador invited Feigenbaum and me to lunch and spent some time querying us about the differences between stakeholder, partner, and shareholder. They wanted to understand how Zoellick's speech related to other approaches to China, such as hedging and balancing. I have been told that the Chinese called others around Washington and that it took some time for the Chinese government to identify the appropriate characters for translating the term "responsible stakeholder." At one point, Feigenbaum prepared, and Zoellick cleared, a formal note walking the Chinese through different manifestations of the concept, which was then shared with the Chinese embassy. At the next high-level meeting between Zoellick and his Chinese counterpart, Vice Foreign Minister Dai Bingguo, the Chinese went to some lengths to point out how they had acted as a responsible stakeholder, noting policies such as their support for UN peacekeeping missions. On the U.S. side, Zoellick walked Dai and others through the implications of the phrase.

The conceptualization of China as a responsible stakeholder did have heuristic punch. It could be applied not only to obvious issues like intellectual property rights, but also to ones that might not immediately be apparent. It could be used to challenge China to weigh policy trade-offs it had hitherto avoided, such as supporting the World Bank as a 4 percent voting stakeholder, on the one hand, while undercutting its loan policies through no-strings bilateral soft loans, on the other. It could be used to persuade China to see its interests in a different light with regard to Sudan or the Extractive Industries Transparency Initiative. Responsible stakeholder provided a framework within which apparently disparate aspects of American policy toward China—the Sudan, raw materials, trade—could be understood as part of a single over-arching coherent approach.

The adoption of the responsible stakeholder concept would appear to be a good example of how a rational policy planning process should work. In fact, the garbage can or policy streams model offers a way of more accurately understanding what actually happened. The confluence of a problem, a solution, and a person was necessary for the United States to adopt this new orientation. The notion of China as a responsible stakeholder had been sitting around in the policy soup, or at least in Evan Feigenbaum's desk drawer, for several years. The conceptualization became policy because the deputy secretary of state opened a policy window. Had the deputy's interests or orientation been different, "responsible stakeholder" would never have entered the lexicon of American foreign policy.

The Partnership for Democratic Governance:
From Academic Idea to Policy Initiative

On October 1, 2007, at an event on the margins of the UN General Assembly meeting, the secretary general of the Organization for Economic Cooperation and Development (OECD), Angel Gurría; the administrator of the UN Development Program (UNDP), Kemal Dervis; the U.S. secretary of state, Condoleezza Rice; the foreign minister of Chile, Alejandro Foxley; and the deputy foreign minister of Poland, Andrzej Sardos, announced the creation of the Partnership for Democratic Governance (PDG). The members of the Partnership were the OECD, the UNDP, Australia, Brazil, Canada, Chile, Denmark, Japan, Korea, Mexico, New Zealand, Poland, Turkey, the United States, the Organization of American States, and the Inter-American Development Bank. A publication issued by the OECD a few months later stated that the "Partnership for Democratic Governance aims to support developing countries . . . in building their governance capacity and improving service delivery to their citizens."[14] The publication indicated that the "PDG Advisory Unit is the operational arm of the Partnership. It collects and shares information on best practices related to contracting out. It carries out country assessments and determines whether, given the country's circumstances, direct provisions of external expertise could deliver results and help build capacity."

The PDG did not have resources to directly fund projects; the Advisory Unit was supported by modest contributions from some of the founding members.

The first glimmer of an idea for the PDG occurred on January 18, 2006, in a van parked outside a building at Georgetown University, where Secretary Rice had given a speech on transformational diplomacy. I was sitting in the van next to Sean McCormack, the assistant secretary of state for public affairs. McCormack suggested that it might be worthwhile for policy planning to explore some possibilities for legacy initiatives for the secretary. The policy planning staff developed possibilities in a variety of areas, including energy and the treatment of orphans. The idea for the PDG came from "Sharing Sovereignty," a paper that I had published in *International Security* in 2004.[15] The basic argument of the paper was that many of the countries around the world vested with international legal sovereignty, and even Westphalian/Vattelian sovereignty, lacked effective domestic sovereignty. In some cases they did not have the capacity to provide services to their own population. In other cases distrust within the polity was so great that it was impossible for political leaders to make credible commitments. The most obvious assistance tools, including governance assistance and short-term UN transitional authorities, might not be adequate. The article concluded that shared sovereignty arrangements in which countries contracted out key activities might be appropriate in some cases.

Was contracting out government service the best idea for supporting better governance in states with weak domestic sovereignty? Not necessarily. Was there some rational decisionmaking process that could have surveyed all of the possibilities for new U.S. multilateral initiatives and provided the secretary of state with the best possible option? I do not think so. But in an environment where democracy and governance were central issues for the administration, it was an idea that had some initial traction.

Turning this idea into reality required buy-in, or at least not outright hostility, from a number of people at the State Department and USAID, support from the secretary of state, and ultimately approval at a principals' meeting in September of 2006. More important, it required support from some other countries and an international home, since no one wanted the PDG to be a free-standing entity. In the summer and fall of 2006 I traveled to Europe, South America, Asia, and Australia to try to sell the idea. Ultimately the PDG did get support from several countries. For me, the most striking was Australia, which was already engaged in an ambitious regional contracting-out project, the Regional Assistance Mission to Solomon Islands (RAMSI). RAMSI was directly involved in running the police, judicial, and financial affairs of the Solomon Islands.

As important as individual country support was getting the backing of the OECD, which ultimately housed the PDG advisory group, and the UNDP. At the OECD, Angel Gurría, the secretary general, was the key figure. Gurría was attentive to new opportunities for the OECD. Moreover, as finance minister in Mexico he had considered contracting out the collection of Mexican customs, something that a number of other countries around the world had done. Although he did not succeed, he was very familiar with the rationale for bringing in external service providers, which in the case of customs was because of the problem of corruption. Kemal Dervis, the administrator of the UNDP, a former finance minister in Turkey and World Bank official, whom I had met when he was working in Washington before taking up his UN position, was also supportive.

Thus the Partnership for Democratic Governance was one of those relatively rare instances in which an academic idea became a policy reality. But the idea itself was hardly enough. Problem recognition and politics were critical. Governance failures in weak states were seen as a problem by officials in the United States and other countries. At the international level, politics also mattered. Some countries, such as Australia, were very familiar with the concept. Others were happy to align themselves with an American initiative, especially one that was not particularly costly. Some countries that declined to join the PDG were skeptical of the idea, and others wanted to distance themselves from the Bush administration. Bargaining as well as persuasion, perhaps bargaining much more than persuasion, is what mattered on the political side.

By early 2008 the PDG advisory unit was set up within the OECD and headed by a very capable Polish diplomat. Interest had been expressed by a number of developing countries. The Economics Bureau at the State Department, which is responsible for U.S. engagement with the OECD, assumed primary responsibility for the PDG. U.S. funding came from the foreign assistance budget.

While many foreign assistance programs go on for years without showing any meaningful success, this will not be the case for the Partnership. Because the Partnership is not embedded within some larger foreign assistance bureaucracy like USAID, it will have to demonstrate its utility. The Advisory Unit will have to identify potential projects and facilitate their implementation, which will mean bringing together recipient country governments, funders, and service providers. If the Partnership had emerged from an operational agency within the U.S. government, such as USAID, the challenges might be fewer, since there would be an entity, at least on the American side, that was prepared to make the Partnership part of its core budget request.

As with the example of China as a responsible stakeholder, the multiple streams or garbage can model provides a framework for understanding policy formulation and implementation. Concern about service delivery in newly democratizing states among those in the political stream in the American government was essential for problem recognition. Political entrepreneurship was facilitated by the policy planning director's access to both the political and policy alternatives streams.

Conclusion

If policy within the American government could be set through a process that vetted all possible alternatives and chose the one that maximized utility, then putting some effort into rationalizing the strategic planning capacity of the government would be worthwhile. If, however, the garbage can or policy streams model provides a more accurate description, then it may be more important to pay attention to the quality and capacity of various planning units rather than trying to organize them more effectively. The planning staffs in different agencies will not always make a contribution to policy formulation. The secretary or national security adviser might not be interested in problems that the planning staff is best able to address. Strategic orientations set early in an administration may be fixed in place because people in the political stream believe that the political cost of changing them is too high regardless of the kinds of strategic alternatives policy planning staffs might formulate.

Nevertheless, there are moments when policy planning staffs can make critical contributions. Their relative independence within the bureaucracy, the mixture of skills possessed by staff members, time to think, an obligation to come up with new ideas, and access to principals provide policy planning with a privileged role within the policy alternatives stream. When policy windows open, planning staffs are at least one promising source from which new solutions can flow. The quality of individuals on these staffs and the access that their directors have to principals will be more important determinants of this contribution than anything that can be achieved by changing organizational structures.

Notes

1. Paul Nitze, "The Implications of Theory for Practice in the Conduct of Foreign Affairs," unpublished paper, 1954, p. 1.

2. Malcolm Gladwell, *Blink: The Power of Thinking without Thinking* (New York: Little, Brown, 2005).

3. Michael Cohen, James March, and Johan Olsen, "A Garbage Can Model of Organizational Choice," *Administrative Science Quarterly* 17 (March 1972): 1.

4. Ibid., p. 2.

5. John Kingdon, *Agendas, Alternatives, and Public Policies*, 2nd ed. (Boston: Addison-Wesley, 1995).

6. Nikolaos Zahariadis, "The Multiple Streams Framework: Structure, Limitations, Prospects," in *Theories of the Policy Process*, edited by P. A. Sabatier (Boulder, Colo.: Westview, 2007).

7. Kingdon, *Agendas, Alternatives, and Public Policies*, pp. 109–13.

8. Ibid., chap. 5.

9. Ibid., chap. 6.

10. Robert Durant and Paul Diehl, "Agendas, Alternatives, and Public Policy: Lessons from the U.S. Foreign Policy Arena," *Journal of Public Policy* 9 (April/June 1989): 179–205.

11. Kingdon, *Agendas, Alternatives, and Public Policies*, chap. 7; Zahariadis, "The Multiple Streams Framework," pp. 73–74.

12. Kingdon, *Agendas, Alternatives, and Public Policies*, chap. 7.

13. Robert Zoellick, "Whither China: From Membership to Responsibility," remarks to the National Committee on U.S. China Relations, New York, September 21, 2005 (www.state.gov/s/d/former/zoellick/rem/53682.htm [December 18, 2008]).

14. OECD, Partnership for Democratic Governance, Advisory Unit (n.d.), *Partnership for Democratic Governance* (www.oecd.org/dataoecd/27/44/39408281.pdf [December 18, 2008]).

15. Stephen D. Krasner, "Sharing Sovereignty: New Institutions for Collapsed and Failing States," *International Security* 29 (Spring 2004): 85–120.

About the Contributors

Daniel W. Drezner is professor of international politics at the Fletcher School of Law and Diplomacy at Tufts University, and a senior editor at the *National Interest*. A recipient of fellowships from the German Marshall Fund of the United States, the Council on Foreign Relations, and Harvard University, he has worked with Civic Education Project, the RAND Corporation, and the U.S. Department of the Treasury. Drezner is the author of *All Politics Is Global: Explaining International Regulatory Regimes* (2007), *U.S. Trade Strategy* (2006), and *The Sanctions Paradox* (1999). A forthcoming title, *An Unclean Slate*, will examine the tangled future of global governance. Drezner has published more than forty journal articles and book chapters, as well as essays in the *New York Times*, *Wall Street Journal*, and *Washington Post*. He is a regular commentator for *Newsweek* International and NPR's *Marketplace*, and keeps a daily blog at Foreignpolicy.com.

Andrew P. N. Erdmann is a management consultant. He works with clients in the retail, energy, and high-tech industries, as well as in the public and nonprofit sectors. Between 2001 and 2005, Erdmann served in foreign policy positions in the U.S. government as a member of the Department of State's policy planning staff, with the Coalition Provisional Authority in Iraq, and on the National Security Council staff as director for Iran, Iraq, and Strategic Planning. In 2006 he served as an expert adviser to the Baker-Hamilton Iraq Study Group. He taught international affairs at Harvard University and George Washington University and has also served as a consultant to the U.S. Army, the Department of Defense, and the Department of State.

Peter Feaver is the Alexander F. Hehmeyer Professor of Political Science and Public Policy at Duke University and director of the Triangle Institute for Security Studies (TISS). From June 2005 to July 2007, Feaver was on leave from Duke and working as the special adviser for strategic planning and institutional reform on the National Security Council staff at the White House. Feaver co-directed (with Bruce Jentleson) a major research project funded by the Carnegie Corporation, "Wielding American Power: Managing Interventions after September 11." Some of his publications include co-author with Christopher Gelpi and Jason Reifler of *Paying the Human Costs of War* (2009), with Susan Wasiolek and Anne Crossman of *Getting the Best Out of College* (2008), and with Christopher Gelpi of *Choosing Your Battles: American Civil-Military Relations and the Use of Force* (2004); and author of *Armed Servants: Agency, Oversight, and Civil-Military Relations* (2003). In 1993–94, Feaver served as director for defense policy and arms control on the National Security Council. He co-moderates a discussion group, Planet War, at washington post.com; and blogs at Shadow Government on ForeignPolicy.com.

Aaron L. Friedberg is professor of politics and international affairs at Princeton University. He is the author of *The Weary Titan: Britain and the Experience of Relative Decline, 1895–1905* (1988) and *In the Shadow of the Garrison State: America's Anti-Statism and Its Cold War Grand Strategy* (2000). Friedberg has been a fellow at the Smithsonian Institution's Woodrow Wilson International Center for Scholars, the Norwegian Nobel Institute, and Harvard University's Center for International Affairs, and has served as a consultant to several agencies of the U.S. government. In 2001–02 he was the first holder of the Henry Alfred Kissinger Chair in Foreign Policy and International Relations at the Library of Congress. From 2003 to 2005 he was a deputy assistant for national security affairs in the Office of the Vice President. He is a member of the Secretary of State's Advisory Committee on Democracy Promotion.

David F. Gordon is head of research at Eurasia Group, a political risk research and consulting firm. For the final year and a half of the George W. Bush administration, he was director of policy planning for Secretary of State Condoleezza Rice. Earlier he served in the Office of the Director of National Intelligence (DNI) as vice chairman of the National Intelligence Council (NIC), as the director of the CIA's Office of Transnational Issues (OTI), and as national intelligence officer for economic and global issues on the NIC. Dr. Gordon's background includes service as a senior fellow and director at the Overseas Development Council, a senior staff member on the Foreign Affairs

Committee of the U.S. House of Representatives, and as the regional economic policy and democracy/governance adviser for the U.S. Agency for International Development in Nairobi, Kenya. He has taught at the University of Michigan, Michigan State University, the College of William and Mary, Princeton University, Georgetown University, and the University of Nairobi. He is the co-editor, with Ian Bremmer and Paul Bracken, of *Managing Strategic Surprise* (2008).

Richard N. Haass is president of the Council on Foreign Relations. Until June 2003 he was director of policy planning for the Department of State, where he was a principal adviser to Secretary of State Colin Powell on a broad range of foreign policy concerns. Previously, Haass was vice president and director of foreign policy studies at the Brookings Institution. He was also special assistant to President George H. W. Bush and senior director for Near East and South Asian affairs on the staff of the National Security Council from 1989 to1993. Haass is the author or editor of eleven books on American foreign policy, including *War of Necessity, War of Choice: A Memoir of Two Iraq Wars.*

William Inboden is senior vice president of the Legatum Institute. Previously he served as senior director for strategic planning on the National Security Council, and at the Department of State as a member of the policy planning staff and a special adviser in the Office of International Religious Freedom. Dr. Inboden was also a Civitas Fellow at the American Enterprise Institute and has worked as a staff member in both the United States Senate and the House of Representatives. He is the author of *Religion and American Foreign Policy, 1945–1960: The Soul of Containment* (2008) and blogs at Shadow Government on ForeignPolicy.com.

Bruce W. Jentleson is professor of public policy and political science at Duke University, where he previously was director of the Terry Sanford Institute of Public Policy. He has served as special assistant to the director of the State Department policy planning staff (1993–94), as a senior foreign policy adviser in the 2000 presidential campaign of Al Gore, and twice as a foreign policy aide in the U.S. Senate. He is the author of numerous articles and books, including *American Foreign Policy: The Dynamics of Choice in the 21st Century* (2007, 3rd ed.); *Strategic Leadership: Framework for a 21st Century National Security Strategy* (co-author, with Anne-Marie Slaughter, Ivo Daalder, James Steinberg, and others); and "America's Hard Sell," in *Foreign Policy* (co-author, with Steven Weber; November/December 2008). He has been a fellow at

Oxford University, the International Institute for Strategic Studies (London), the Brookings Institution, and the U.S. Institute of Peace and was a Fulbright senior research scholar in Spain.

Stephen D. Krasner is the Graham H. Stuart Professor of International Relations at Stanford University, a senior fellow at the Freeman Spogli Institute, and a senior fellow at the Hoover Institution. He was director of the policy planning staff at the Department of State (2005–07) and director for governance and development at the National Security Council (2002). In 2003–04 he was deputy director of the Freeman Spogli Institute and director of the Center for Democracy, Development and the Rule of Law at the institute, as well as a member of the board of directors of the U.S. Institute of Peace. He is the author of several books, including *Sovereignty: Organized Hypocrisy* (1999), and more than eighty articles. He is a fellow of the American Academy of Arts and Sciences and a member of the Council on Foreign Relations.

Jeffrey W. Legro is Compton Professor of World Politics and chair of the Department of Politics at the University of Virginia. He is co-founder and associate of the Governing America in a Global Era Program at the Miller Center of Public Affairs. He is the author of *Rethinking the World: Great Power Strategies and International Order* (2005) and *Cooperation under Fire: Anglo-German Restraint during World War II* (1995), and a contributor to *The Culture of National Security* (1996). He is the editor, with Melvyn Leffler, of *To Lead the World: U.S. Strategy after the Bush Doctrine* (2008).

Daniel Twining is senior fellow for Asia at the German Marshall Fund of the United States. During the George W. Bush administration, he served as a member of Secretary of State Condoleezza Rice's policy planning staff, with responsibility for South Asia and regional issues in East Asia. He previously worked for over a decade for Senator John McCain, including as his foreign policy adviser in the United States Senate. Previously he was a Fulbright/Oxford scholar at Oxford University, a transatlantic fellow and director of the Foreign Policy Program at the German Marshall Fund of the United States, and a staff member in the Office of the U.S. Trade Representative. His work on South and East Asia and U.S. foreign policy has been published in newspapers, magazines, and academic journals in the United States, Europe, and Asia; he blogs on *Foreign Policy* magazine's Shadow Government website. Mr. Twining was educated at Balliol College, Oxford; Nuffield College, Oxford;

and the University of Virginia. He lived and worked in India in 2006–07 and has also lived in Southeast Asia, Europe, and Africa.

Thomas Wright is executive director of studies at the Chicago Council on Global Affairs. Previously he was senior researcher for the Princeton Project on National Security, a postdoctoral research fellow at the Princeton Institute for International and Regional Studies, and a predoctoral research fellow at Harvard University's Belfer Center for Science and International Affairs. He has published in the *American Political Science Review*, the *Washington Post*, and various international newspapers.

Amy B. Zegart is an associate professor in the School of Public Affairs at UCLA and a visiting fellow at the Hoover Institution, Stanford University. She served on the Clinton administration's National Security Council staff in 1993, has provided intelligence training to the Marine Corps and the Office of the Director of National Intelligence, and has advised local, state, and federal officials on intelligence and homeland security issues. She is the author of *Flawed by Design: The Evolution of the CIA, JCS, and NSC* (1999) and *Spying Blind: The CIA, the FBI, and the Origins of 9/11* (2007), which won the 2008 Brownlow Book Award, the top literary prize given by the National Academy of Public Administration. Before pursuing an academic career, Zegart spent three years as a management consultant at McKinsey & Company. She is a member of the Council on Foreign Relations and California's Homeland Security Advisory Council.

Index

180 *Index*

Brazil: and international economic development, 49; and international trade, 47; and PDG, 168

Bremer Commission, 119

Bretton Woods, 127, 128, 134

Brimley, Shawn, 3

Brin, Sergey, 144

British Petroleum, 141

Browne, Lord, 141

Brzezinski, Zbigniew, 74, 89

Buchanan, Pat, 58–59

Bureaucracy: and integrative executive branch strategy, 73–75, 78–79; and political pressures, 90; as strategic planning obstacle, 88–90; and turf battles, 117–19

Bush, George H. W., 47, 91

Bush, George W.: and AIM foreign policy, 52, 56, 64; and China diplomacy, 42; and global war on terror, 9, 100; and idealist foreign policy, 30; and international economic development, 47; and 9/11 response, 116, 125; NSC role under, 74–75; and policy implementation, 121; and strategic planning, 4, 8–9, 96; and U.S. disengagement from multilateral organizations, 132; Washington Islamic Center speech by, 102

Bush doctrine, 6, 15, 52, 54–55, 63

Cadbury Schweppes, 144

Capacity for strategic planning, 84–97

Capitalism, 45

Cardinal Health, 144

Carter, Jimmy, 91

Causal connections, 71

Central Intelligence Agency (CIA): creation of, 96; and NSC Planning Board, 74; short-term focus of, 115; and turf battles, 117

Chan Heng Chee, 42

Chief strategy officer (CSO), role in private sector, 149

China: and AIM foreign policy, 52, 61–62; bilateral relations with, 42, 131; as garbage can framework example, 165–68; and globalization, 46, 48; and integration doctrine, 29; and international trade, 47; and nonpolarity of world power, 26; as partner and rival, 130; power and influence of, 6–7, 41–43; strategic planning on, 85

Christopher, Warren, 31

Churchill, Winston, 128

CIA. *See* Central Intelligence Agency

C-level executives, 149

Climate change: foreign policy challenges of, 29; and globalization, 47–48; and India-U.S. diplomacy, 43; and institutional reform, 133; and nonpolarity of world power, 27; and NSS, 80; and Obama administration, 28; and political constraints, 79, 91

Clinton, Bill: and foreign policy planning, 3–4, 9; and international economic development, 47; NSC role under, 74; and policy implementation, 121

Cognitive limitations, 92, 120–21, 159

Cohen, Michael, 160–61

Cohen, William, 81

Cold war: diplomacy during, 130–31; and foreign policy shifts, 53, 54; and Kennan's containment strategy, 34–35; strategic planning for, 96; and timing of policy planning, 25

"Command Strategy 2016," 10

Commerce Department, 74, 76, 88, 118

Community of Democracies project, 12

Conceptualization of strategies, 71

Congress, electoral cycles of, 75

Containment doctrine: development of, 114, 160; implementation of, 165;